Seasonal SPECIALS for Children's Ministry

All-NEW ideas for **13** holidays

Group

Loveland, Colorado
group.com

Group resources really work!

This Group resource incorporates our R.E.A.L. approach to ministry. It reinforces a growing friendship with Jesus, encourages long-term learning, and results in life transformation, because it's

Relational
Learner-to-learner interaction enhances learning and builds Christian friendships.

Experiential
What learners experience through discussion and action sticks with them up to 9 times longer than what they simply hear or read.

Applicable
The aim of Christian education is to equip learners to be both hearers and doers of God's Word.

Learner-based
Learners understand and retain more when the learning process takes into consideration how they learn best.

Seasonal Specials for Children's Ministry

Copyright © 2012 Group Publishing, Inc.

Visit our website: **group.com**

Credits

Contributing Authors: Lisa Bartelt, Jody Brolsma, E.C. Cunningham, Dawn Rundman, RoseAnne Sather, Patty Smith, Sharon Stratmoen, Adam Walsh, Courtney Walsh, Amy Weaver

(The Easter skit, "The Box of Stones," was written by Rick Clark and used by permission.)

Editors: Ann Diaz, Jennifer Hooks, Ali Thompson, Adam Walsh, Christine Yount Jones, Andrea Zimmerman

Cover Art Directors: Rebecca Parrott, Joey Vining

Interior Art Director: Jean Bruns

Illustrators: Mernie Gallagher-Cole (Portfolio Solutions, LLC), Kate Elvin, Rebecca Parrott, RoseAnne Sather

Production Artist: Suzi Jensen

ISBN 978-0-7644-7991-5

10 9 8 7 6 5 4 3 2   18 17 16 15 14 13 12

Printed in the United States of America.

Contents

Introduction

Sunday morning often revolves around what's happening during the year, holiday-wise. If kids are decorating red hearts with 1 Corinthians 13:13 stickers, Valentine's Day is probably around the corner. Painting a flower pot? Mother's Day, for sure. And for those who minister to children, the holidays can be the hardest times to find fresh, faith-focused ideas.

That's where *Seasonal Specials* comes in.

We've set about celebrating 13 popular holidays—all from a Christian perspective. You and preschoolers through preteens can blow out each holiday with a devotion, craft, skit, snack, game, song, and outreach idea. That means right now you're holding more than 90 original, innovative, engaging ideas—all stamped with Group's R.E.A.L. Guarantee that these holidays will be more than just a bolded date on a calendar. Instead, they'll be Jesus-centered experiences.

This book covers all the major holidays (Easter, Independence Day, Halloween, Thanksgiving, Christmas, and New Year's Day) as well as other celebrations (Earth Day, Memorial Day, and more). Each holiday's section has fresh ideas that inspire, educate, and celebrate.

You'll find the holidays arranged chronologically, so finding exactly what you're looking for is a cinch. You can use an entire section as a full lesson, or simply pick and choose elements to add to a lesson. Here's an example of the elements you'll find in each chapter.

NEW YEAR'S DAY

Pressing On (Devotion)
New Year's Crackers (Craft)
Do-Over (Game)
New Life Gingerbread People (Snack)
A Clean Heart (Skit)
Jesus Makes All of Us New (Song)
Book Beginnings (Outreach)

Each element includes Scripture, age recommendations, supplies needed, easy-to-follow instructions, and great questions aimed at helping kids explore what they experience.

Jesus used what was around him to teach people about God—including daily life and seasons. He told parables about the harvest, fig trees, and mustard seeds, all in conjunction with what was happening on the calendar. *Seasonal Specials* is designed to follow that model, while making holidays incredibly special—and meaningful—for kids.

Be aware that some children have food allergies that can be dangerous. Know your children, and consult with parents about allergies their children may have. Also be sure to read food labels carefully as hidden ingredients can cause allergy-related problems.

New Year's Day

New Year's Day...new beginnings...a collective do-over. It's the time of year for genuine reflection, slate-wiping, and, interestingly enough, oatmeal. (January is National Oatmeal Month...a good start-your-morning resolution to begin!) As you celebrate a new year, kids will discover how, through Jesus, they're new creations...blank blackboards, ready for God to chalk some love on their hearts.

PRESSING ON

BEST
Elementary
FOR

Kids will learn to move on from the past and press forward for Jesus!

SCRIPTURE

Philippians 3:13-14

WHAT YOU'LL NEED

• Bible
• a sign with last year's date
• a sign with this year's date
• tape

The Experience

Hang your signs on opposite walls, and clear the area between the walls of any obstacles.

Have kids face last year's sign.

SAY: **Let's reflect on the past year. Raise your hand if you've done what I call out.**

• **Who went to a different state last year?**

• **Who got a new brother or sister last year?**

• **Who did something you were proud of last year?**

• **Who did something you regret in the last year?**

SAY: **We've all done things we regret. Maybe we did something embarrassing, or maybe we really hurt someone by our actions. Sometimes the memories of those regrets stick in our minds and make us feel bad. Getting stuck on what we did in the past can really mess up how we feel about the future. I'll show you what I mean.**

Have kids continue facing last year's wall and walk until they're standing right up against it.

SAY: **Your goal is to race across the room, but you have to walk backward, keeping your eyes on last year. If you bump into anyone, fall down, or peek behind you, you have to sit right where you**

are, so be careful! Allow a few minutes for kids to play. Declare the winner and then have kids sit in a circle.

ASK: **What was hard about racing backward?**

• **Tell about a time you were focused on a mistake or bad choice you made—and it caused a problem for you.**

• **How can remembering our bad choices help or hurt our future?**

SAY: **It's good to learn from the things we've done wrong. But when we hold onto guilt or bad feelings, we forget that God has forgiven us. We can get stuck in the past, thinking God doesn't love us anymore. But the Bible has something important to say about holding onto the past as we go through life.** Read Philippians 3:13-14.

Have kids all start back at last year's wall.

SAY: **Let's put this verse into practice. Rather than focusing on what's behind us (last year), let's look toward what's ahead. Turn around and race toward the sign for the new year. Ready? Go!**

When all the kids are at the new sign, declare them all winners.

ASK: **What does it mean to "press on" for God?**

• **How can you live for Jesus this year?**

SAY: **A lot of people make resolutions on New Year's Day. We vow to do things such as get more exercise, read more, or eat healthier foods. Those are all good goals. But the most important goal we have is a lifelong one: to live for Jesus. If we live every day with our eyes focused on him, we'll have fewer regrets each year. And we'll also know that Jesus forgives us for the wrong things we do when we ask him to. So don't dwell in the past—just keep your eyes on what Jesus has in store for you this year!**

Craft

NEW YEAR'S CRACKERS

BEST All Ages FOR

Kids will make a traditional New Year's craft as a reminder to live for Jesus in the new year.

SCRIPTURE

Ephesians 5:15-16

ALLERGY ALERT *See p. 7*

WHAT YOU'LL NEED

- Bible
- paper towel or wrapping paper tubes cut to 12 inches
- colorful paper
- metallic pens
- safety scissors
- colorful tissue paper
- metallic ribbon
- candy
- clear tape
- shiny stickers

The Experience

Before kids arrive, cut tissue paper into 12-inch by 20-inch strips. Cut metallic curling ribbon into 12-inch lengths. Cut colorful paper into 1x4-inch strips. For younger kids, write or print the words from Ephesians 5:15-16 on the strips of paper.

SAY: **Happy New Year! People around the globe celebrate the arrival of a new year with lots of traditions.**

ASK: **What New Year's traditions does your family have?**

SAY: **All over the world, people celebrate New Year's Eve and New Year's Day. In England, they share something called party crackers. Party crackers are tubes that make a big pop when you open them. Inside you'll find a message, treats, and a paper hat that looks like a crown. We're going to make our own New Year's crackers with an important message to** share about how to live for Jesus in the coming year.

First, **we'll work on our message. There's a great Bible verse that can help us know how to live for Jesus this year.** Read aloud Ephesians 5:15-16. Pass out the slips of colorful paper and help kids each write this verse on a slip using metallic markers. Then have them tuck the papers in their paper towel tubes.

ASK: **What do you think this verse means?**

• **What does it mean to "make the most of every opportunity"?**

SAY: **Now let's make a paper crown to tuck inside. This is part of the English tradition— people all wear the hat they find inside the cracker! Our crowns can remind us that when Jesus is king of our lives, we live for him.**

Show kids how to cut out a piece of tissue paper that will fit around their heads with a few extra inches left to overlap and tape. They can cut scalloped designs along the top to look more crownlike. When they're done, have kids gently fold the hats to fit into the tubes.

Help kids wrap their tubes with tissue paper and tie one end with curling ribbon. Then have kids put some candy in the tubes along with the paper slips and crowns before tying off the other end. Kids can decorate the outside of the tubes with metallic markers or stickers.

SAY: **Take your party cracker home with you. As you celebrate New Year's this year, crack it open. Read the verse and enjoy the sweet candy** with your family as you pray for God's help in making the most of every opportunity in the coming year.

DO-OVER

Kids either get a "do-over"— or they don't—when aiming paper airplanes at a target.

SCRIPTURE

2 Corinthians 5:17

WHAT YOU'LL NEED

- sheets of paper
- masking tape

The Experience

Give each child a sheet of paper to fold it into a paper airplane. (For younger kids, demonstrate how to make a paper airplane or let kids just crumple their papers and throw them like a ball.) Once kids have created their planes, use masking tape to make a square target on the floor several feet away.

SAY: **The goal of this game is to land your airplane or ball inside the square.** Without allowing any time to practice, have kids take turns trying to land their airplane or ball inside the tape square. If the plane lands right side up, say, "Do-over!" and let the child try again until he or she hits the target or the plane lands upside down. (If kids are throwing balls, allow every other child who misses a do-over.) If a child's plane lands upside down, that child doesn't get another chance. However, don't explain *why* certain kids get a do-over and others don't until the end of the game. Note: Kids may get frustrated that some people get a second chance and others don't; that's okay—it's part of the experience. If you have time, play again.

ASK: **What does it mean to get a do-over?**

• **How did you react when you either got or didn't get a do-over in this game?**

• **Talk about a time someone gave you a do-over in your life.**

• **If you could have one do-over in real life, what would you do over and why?**

SAY: **New Year's Day is a time to remember the past and look forward to the future. It's a fresh start and a chance to do-over the things we've messed up. God offered us the biggest do-over ever when he sent Jesus. Because Jesus died for us, we get a second chance. In 2 Corinthians 5:17, the Bible says that anyone who belongs to Christ has become a new person. Out with the old, and in with the new! Our sins are wiped away, like wiping clean a chalkboard. We can start fresh. Let's fly into the New Year thanking God for giving us a second chance.**

Snack

NEW LiFe GiNGeRbReaD PeOPLe

BEST All Ages FOR

Kids discover that no matter how messy life gets, they get a new start with Jesus.

ALLERGY ALERT *See p. 7*

SCRIPTURE

2 Corinthians 5:17

WHAT YOU'LL NEED

- Bible
- 1 gingerbread person per child
- paper plates
- plastic knives
- white frosting
- Bugles snacks
- Fruity Pebbles cereal
- M&M's candies or yogurt-covered raisins
- plastic spoons

The Experience

Give each child a gingerbread person on a paper plate, and set out the supplies.

SAY: **Use the supplies to decorate your gingerbread person. But you have to do it with your eyes closed.** Allow time; then have kids open their eyes.

ASK: **What do you think of your gingerbread creation?**

• **How does a messy gingerbread person remind you of what we feel like when we've done something wrong?**

SAY: **The Bible says we've all done wrong things. On the inside, we've all looked like a messy gingerbread person. But listen to this!** Read aloud 2 Corinthians 5:17.

SAY: **Let's make our gingerbread people into new people, just like Jesus did for us. As we start this new year, we can celebrate our new life in Jesus.** Have kids scrape off their frosting and decorations. Then have kids keep their eyes open and redecorate their gingerbread people.

Have kids put a Bugle "party horn" in the gingerbread person's mouth to remind them to celebrate new life in Jesus. Then let kids eat their gingerbread people.

ASK: **How will you live life differently this year knowing that Jesus made you a new person?**

SAY: **All we need to do is ask, and we'll belong to Jesus. That means we're new people! Remembering what Jesus has done for us can help us remember to live like we're new this year.**

A CLEAN HeaRt

BEST
All Ages
FOR

Kate learns how God erases sin.

Scripture

Psalm 51:10

Props

- a chair
- a stethoscope (toy or real)
- a large ball
- black tape

Cast

- Jesus
- Kate

Behind the Scenes

This is a simple setup with just a chair for Kate, set on one side of the stage. Kate holds a ball with two black strips of tape stuck to it. Jesus wears a stethoscope.

 *Action!*

➡ *Kate sits in the chair. She's waiting, and has a large ball covered with strips of black tape in her hands. Jesus enters with a stethoscope around his neck.*

JESUS

Okay...Kate? Is Kate out here?

KATE

That's me.

JESUS

You're up next!

My notes say you have questions about your heart.

➡ *Kate stands. She starts to hold out her ball with the black tape on it, but she pulls back. She's a bit hesitant.*

KATE

Yes, but...I'm not sure what's going to happen.

JESUS

Oh?

➡ *Kate looks at the ball.*

KATE

My mom says God looks at our hearts. And I'm not so sure mine is okay. She says he forgives us if we do something wrong—just wipes our heart clean.

JESUS

Right. Your mom's one smart cookie.

KATE

But I don't get it.

JESUS

It's just like she says. Wiped clean. Kind of like a do-over. Like New Year's Day, new year, new things, starting over...like that.

KATE

So, if I do something wrong, and I ask God to forgive me, then that thing I did just...goes away?

JESUS

Well, yes. He forgives you. Gone. Adios.

➡ *Kate hands the ball to Jesus.*

KATE

Will it hurt?

➡ *Jesus smiles, reassuring Kate.*

JESUS

It might. There might be things you don't want to admit or don't want to talk about. Are you ready?

➡ *Kate looks at Jesus as if to say, "Do I have to?" Jesus nods and smiles. He points to a specific piece of black tape.*

JESUS

Let's start here. What's this one?

KATE

(Hesitant) I lied to my mom.

JESUS

Oooh. Not the best idea. Hold still.

➡ *Kate stands completely still, eyes shut in a wince, as if waiting for something to hurt. Jesus pulls off the tape in one swift motion, as if quickly pulling off a bandage. Kate slowly peeks out of one eye at Jesus.*

KATE

That...wasn't that bad.

JESUS

Great! But...that's not all of it. Your heart still looks like this. *(He points to another piece.)* What about this one?

KATE

That one I don't really want to talk about. It's going to hurt.

JESUS

God wants to help you with everything, Kate. Even the hard stuff.

KATE

Well, I'm not forgiving him! He did it on purpose!

JESUS

If you don't forgive your brother, then God can't forgive you.

KATE

But he hurt my feelings! He made fun of me in front of my friends!

JESUS

I know it's hard. Maybe you want to get back at him. But that's not how God does it.

KATE

But my brother was wrong!

JESUS

And you still need to forgive him. *(Pauses.)* Are you ready?

➡ *Kate gives a big sigh. She looks at Jesus.*

JESUS

Remember, it'll be like New Year's Day every day.

KATE

(Grimacing) New Year's Day every day...

JESUS

Fresh start. Clean heart. Just like New Year's. Ready?

KATE

Ready.

➡ *Jesus pulls off the piece of black tape. Kate winces like it hurt a bit, but then breathes easier.*

KATE

Wow. I feel a lot better. You were right. Thanks.

➡ *Kate turns and starts to leave.*

JESUS

I'll be here to help whenever you need me. Oh, Kate?

KATE

Yes?

JESUS

Here's your heart back. Good as new.

➡ *Jesus hands Kate the ball. Both smile.*

JESUS MAKES ALL OF US NEW

BEST *Preschool* **FOR**

Kids dance and sing as they give everything to Jesus, to the tune of the "Mexican Hat Dance!"

SCRIPTURE

2 Corinthians 5:17

Sing It!

When we give all our heart to *(Kids jump and shout)* **Jesus!**

When we give all our mind to *(Kids jump and shout)* **Jesus!**

When we give all our soul to *(Kids jump and shout)* **Jesus!**

Jesus makes all of us new!

And then Jesus will give you a new life *(Kids do-si-do around each other, arms linked)*

And then Jesus will give you a new life

And then Jesus will give you a new life

Jesus makes all of us new! *(Kids throw arms up in air.)*

BOOK BEGINNINGS

BEST
Elementary
FOR

Books will get new life as kids replace tarnished covers.

SCRIPTURE

Isaiah 43:18-19

WHAT YOU'LL NEED

- Bible
- clear packing tape
- brown paper grocery bags, brown shipping paper, or wrapping paper
- scissors
- staplers
- cotton swabs
- rubber bands
- glue
- markers
- stickers
- clear contact paper

The Experience

In early to mid-December, publicize your need for donations of worn, tattered, and used children's books. Set up a box at church or school (with the school's permission) to collect the books. Establish a cut-off date for donations a week before you intend to make repairs on the books. Also, find a children's reading group in your community. Many communities have programs through the library, school, or other charitable organizations to help kids practice reading.

Sort the donated books by the repair they need—such as torn covers, loose spines, loose pages, missing covers, and so on.

Sit in a circle and <u>SAY</u>: **A new year means new beginnings—a great time for a fresh start! Here's what God has to say about new beginnings.** Read Isaiah 43:18-19. **Today we're going to give some books new beginnings. We'll repair their covers, and then find new homes for them.**

Divide tasks, according to age group if necessary. Repair the books as needed.

Loose pages, depending on the type of book, can be reattached by stapling, taping, or gluing. When using glue to reattach pages or covers, use cotton swabs for tight places, such as bindings. Then wrap rubber bands around the books and let them sit overnight.

For torn and missing covers, let the kids have fun decorating their own replacement covers using the paper bags and wrapping paper. Follow these steps for making new covers for books.

1. If using paper bags, cut them so they lay flat. Cut from a top corner straight to the bottom, and then around three sides of the base of the bag. Then cut off the base and lay the bag flat. If kids will decorate the outside, make sure the plain side is facing down. If using wrapping paper or a roll of shipping paper, roll out a large piece and lay it flat.

2. Choose a book and lay it in the center of the bag or paper. Fold the bottom up to meet the edge of the book, and crease the paper or bag. Repeat at the top. Remove the book and finish the fold so you have two pieces the length of the paper folded over at the top and the bottom.

3. Place the book in the center of the paper, on top of the folds, and position it until the left and right sides appear to be equal. Fold paper over the front cover so both sides are even.

4. Fold the left side over and inside the front cover. If the paper is too long, trim so it covers about three-fourths of the inside cover. Insert the cover into the flap made by the folds. Close and pull the paper tight around the front cover.

5. Repeat Step 4 for the back cover. Fold the right side over and inside the back cover. Trim if necessary. Insert the back cover into the flap.

6. Decorate the outside with markers, crayons, and stickers. Don't forget to include the title of the book! Reinforce the cover with clear contact paper or by sticking tape to the inside flaps.

Extra Special FACTOIDS

DID YOU KNOW...

The ancient Babylonians were the first to make New Year's resolutions... about 4,000 years ago. Their most common vows for the new year? To "return borrowed farm equipment and pay off old debts."

DID YOU KNOW...

Tampering with the calendar had become common practice in various societies. In 153 B.C., the Roman senate declared a fresh start: January 1 would begin the new year. In 46 B.C., Julius Caesar declared another do-over but had to extend that year to 445 days to synchronize the calendar with the sun.

Valentine's Day

Heart-shaped chocolate boxes and pink teddy bears overstuff the stores this time of year, as romance flourishes through gift-giving and odes of affection. But there's a love much greater than romantic love between valentines: God's unconditional, eternal love. And best of all, God extends his love to everyone. As you celebrate Valentine's Day, help kids celebrate the greatest love of all...and learn how they can share God's message with others.

Devotion

Love Letters

BEST FOR
Upper Elementary

Kids dig into God's sweet love for them and offer their love in return.

Scripture

1 John 4:7-12

What You'll Need

- Bible
- large bowl
- candy conversation hearts
- paper
- pens

ALLERGY ALERT See p. 7

The Experience

Have kids wash their hands. SAY: **Valentine's Day is a day when we tell others how much we love and appreciate them. We might do this by sending our friends cards, giving people candy, or telling others how we feel about them. Let's see what the Bible says about expressing our love for others.**

Have kids form a circle. Pour the candy hearts into a large bowl and place it in the center of the circle. Explain to kids that every time they hear the word *love* in the passage, each child can take one candy heart from the bowl. But every time they hear the word *not*, everyone has to put one heart back in the bowl.

Read aloud 1 John 4:7-12, pausing to allow kids time to take candy or put it back in the bowl. When you're done reading the passage, each child should have 10 candy hearts.

ASK: **Put one heart back, and tell about a time you needed God's love.**

- **Eat one of your candy hearts, and tell how God has shown his love for you.**
- **What do these verses teach us about *real* love?**

SAY: **On Valentine's Day we focus on loving others. It's important that we express our love for others; that pleases God. Most important, we want to show our love for the One who loves us most—God. He shows us his love in so many ways. So let's create a Valentine's Day card to tell God how we feel about him.**

Give each child a pen and a sheet of paper. Encourage kids to fold the paper in half to create a card. Then have kids write a love letter to God while finding a creative way to include their conversation candy hearts into the letter. Rather than writing the words, kids can set their candy conversation hearts on the appropriate parts of the letter.

Once kids have each completed a love letter, encourage them to read theirs aloud to the group. Then have everyone enjoy the candy as you discuss the following question.

ASK: **What are some ways you can show your love for God this week?**

SAY: **Just as you expressed your love for God in a letter, God tells us how he feels about us in his love letter, the Bible. That's where we can read about how he showed his love for us by sending Jesus to take the punishment for our sins. This Valentine's Day, let's celebrate God's love by remembering what he's done for us and by loving those around us.**

We Love Tambourines

BEST All Ages FOR

Kids make tambourines to celebrate that God's faithful love endures forever.

SCRIPTURE

Psalm 136:1-3

WHAT YOU'LL NEED

- Bible
- paper plates, 2 per child
- jingle bells
- small, solid objects such as beads, buttons, or soda tabs
- staplers
- hole punches
- yarn
- markers
- scraps of pink, purple, and red tissue paper
- Mod Podge sealer
- paintbrushes

The Experience

Read aloud Psalm 136:1-3. <u>SAY:</u> **This Psalm praises God and thanks him for all he's done to show his love. We're going to celebrate what God's done to show love to us. But first, we need some rhythm!**

Hand out paper plates. Help kids staple around the edges, about one inch from the edge, leaving a small opening at the top. Pour about a quarter cup of beads or buttons into each set of plates, and then help kids staple the hole shut.

Use a hole punch to make three holes around the edges of the plates, outside the stapled circles. Have kids tie a piece of yarn through each hole and attach jingle bells.

For younger kids, draw a large heart on each side of the plate, and have kids color their hearts with markers. Have older kids draw hearts and then use a paintbrush to fill in the hearts with Mod Podge sealer. Let kids arrange scraps of tissue paper on the sealer to create a stained-glass look. When they're done adding tissue paper, they'll need to apply another layer of Mod Podge sealer.

Have kids stand in a circle. <u>SAY:</u> **Now let's make up our own praise chant like the one in Psalm 136. We'll go around the circle and each chant one thing we're thankful for. When it's your turn, shake your tambourine while you share. Then we'll all shake our tambourines and say, "His faithful love endures forever!"**

Go around the circle once; then let kids add additional things.

Balloon Buddies

Kids try not to "let down" their buddies in this hands-off, high-energy game.

SCRIPTURE

Psalm 36:5-9

WHAT YOU'LL NEED

- Bible
- 1 balloon per person
- permanent markers for older kids
- garbage bag

The Experience

Hand each child a balloon, and have kids inflate and tie off their balloons. Let each person draw a simple face on his or her balloon. Then gather the balloons into a garbage bag.

Have kids link arms to make a circle. Hold up one balloon, and SAY: **In this game, we'll see how long we can keep our friend here off the ground. If you let this balloon buddy touch the ground, we'll have to start again.**

Explain that kids can use their heads, knees, bodies, or feet to keep the balloon off the ground…but they can't use their hands (since their arms are linked). Toss the balloon into the middle of the circle to start the game. After 30 seconds, SAY: **Let's add a little more challenge.** Add a second balloon and play again.

After another 30 seconds, SAY: **Okay, now I know you're ready for a *big* challenge.** Toss all the balloons in the middle of the circle and see if kids can keep them off the ground. Allow 60 chaotic seconds as kids try to keep the balloons off the ground.

Then collect the balloons, and ASK:

- **On a scale of 1 to 5—with 1 being lousy and 5 being perfect—how good were you at keeping our balloon buddies off the ground? Why did you rate yourself that way?**
- **What was hard about keeping the balloons in the air?**

SAY: **Sometimes in real life, people let us down. People might break promises or forget to do something. Find a partner, and tell about a time someone disappointed you or let you down.** Allow a few minutes for kids to share.

Read aloud Psalm 36:5-9, and ASK:

- **What does "unfailing love" mean to you?**
- **How would you show someone else unfailing love?**
- **What is one example of God's unfailing love in *your* life?**

SAY: **In our game, we let the balloon people down—literally! But God's love never fails; he never lets us down! God holds each of us tenderly and lovingly in his arms always, no matter what. This Valentine's Day, you can truly celebrate because you know God loves you!**

Warning! To avoid choking hazards, be sure to pick up pieces of any broken balloons promptly. Balloons may contain latex.

Strawberry Surprise

BEST
Elementary
FOR

This fizzy drink is bursting with Valentine's Day love.

ALLERGY ALERT (See p. 7)

SCRIPTURE

1 Thessalonians 3:12

WHAT YOU'LL NEED

- Bible
- vanilla ice cream
- strawberry soda
- strawberry syrup
- strawberry Pop Rocks candy
- 8-ounce plastic cups
- straws
- tablespoons
- ice cream scoopers

The Experience

SAY: **One way we celebrate Valentine's Day is by telling the special people in our lives how much we love them. Turn to a partner and tell about someone you love. What's your favorite way to show that person you love him or her?**

Allow time, and then invite a few children to share with the entire group.

Give each child a plastic cup. Help kids fill the cups about one-third full with strawberry soda. Then have kids add one tablespoon of strawberry syrup and stir. Next have them add one scoop of ice cream. Pause and let kids observe what happens.

SAY: **When we add the soda to the ice cream, carbon dioxide moves out of the soda solution and clusters around the air bubbles in the ice cream. This causes the air bubbles to grow and expand, creating the fizzy, foamy drink.**

ASK: **How are the growing bubbles like God's love?**

SAY: **Let's see what the Bible says about loving others.**

Read 1 Thessalonians 3:12.

SAY: **God loves us so much that his love can overflow out of our lives, helping us love others.** Have kids add more strawberry soda to their cups.

ASK: **How is what happened to your soda like this verse?**

• **Why do you think God's love for us makes our love for others grow and grow?**

• **What are ways others can *see* God's love through you?**

Have kids sprinkle Pop Rocks candy on top of their sodas and listen.

ASK: **What are ways others can *hear* God's love through you?**

Distribute straws to kids and let them enjoy their sodas.

Valentine's Day

Unexpected Valentine

BEST
All Ages
FOR

After a rough day at school, Lucy finds a surprise valentine in a mailbox.

SCRIPTURE

Genesis 1:1

PROPS

- a red mailbox (or just a red box)
- a letter in an envelope
- a chair

CAST

- Mom
- Lucy
- Male Narrator

BEHIND THE SCENES

The simple setup is just a chair at the right of the stage, with a red mailbox or box placed beside it. Place the letter that Lucy will take out and read later in the skit inside the box. The letter can be decorated however you wish.

 **Action!**

➡ *The scene begins with no actors upfront. The Narrator speaks from offstage and addresses everyone in the room.*

NARRATOR

Has anyone ever had a rough day? *(Pause.)* Turn to the person next to you and tell about a rough day you had recently.

➡ *Allow about two minutes, and then continue.*

NARRATOR

When you have a rough day, it can feel as if no one loves you. After your rough day, you might've felt something like this...

➡ *Mom is standing on the opposite side of the stage from the chair. Lucy walks in, and she's depressed. She had a rough day at school.*

MOM

Hey, sweetie! How was school? Wasn't today your Valentine's Day party?

LUCY

(Lucy shrugs.) Today Jeannie told me the only reason anyone gave me any valentines was because they *had* to.

MOM

Well, that wasn't a very nice thing to say.

LUCY

But she's right. No one wants to give me anything because no one likes anything about me.

MOM

Oh, honey, that's not true. You're amazing.

LUCY

You have to say that. You're my mom.

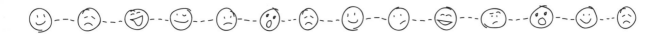

MOM

Lucy, I'm sorry you feel that way. Let me finish dinner, and we'll talk about this more.

➡ *Mom exits and Lucy walks over and slumps in the chair. She looks down and notices the mailbox and frowns, as if it's not supposed to be there.*

LUCY

Mom! Did you put this mailbox here?

➡ *There's no answer. Lucy shrugs and then opens the mailbox. Inside, she finds a letter. She sits in the chair, a confused look still on her face. She opens the letter and as she reads, we hear a voice.*

NARRATOR

Dear Lucy, Happy Valentine's Day. This is a day to celebrate love...and you are very loved.

➡ *Lucy scoffs.*

NARRATOR

What's the matter? Don't you believe me?

➡ *Lucy looks around, shocked that the voice seems to respond to her.*

NARRATOR

You *are* loved. Not just by your parents and friends—but especially by me. I knew you before you were born. I marvelously made you, I watched you being formed—and you're growing up wonderfully.

LUCY

Huh?

NARRATOR

I was so proud of you the other day when that little boy on the playground wanted a chance on the swings and you got up and gave him yours. *(Lucy looks surprised, as if to say, "You saw me there?")* And yesterday when your mom had such a bad day, you jumped in to help with dinner and then unloaded the dishwasher and finished your homework...all without complaining. *(Lucy looks down at her feet, smiling, a bit embarrassed.)* That made me smile. Those pictures you draw...the ones your mom hangs on the fridge? *(Lucy looks up.)* Those are beautiful, and I love how happy you are when you're painting.

LUCY

They *do* make me happy.

NARRATOR

It's one of your gifts...and when you use it, it makes me very happy. I love so many things about you...not just on Valentine's Day, but every day...because I made you to be very special. No matter what anyone else says.

LUCY

Are you sure you know who you're talking to?

NARRATOR

Lucy Jenkins. Age 10. Blonde hair, big brown eyes. Crooked teeth. Loves to sing and dance and paint beautiful pictures. Sometimes worries no one likes her, sometimes forgets to show others her sweet side. Talks to me at night before she goes to bed. Oh, I know who I'm talking about. Lucy Jenkins—you are loved.

LUCY

Thanks, God. Happy Valentine's Day.

➡ *Lucy exits.*

NARRATOR

And it's not just Lucy who's loved. It's everyone in this room. No matter how rough your day is, no matter how you feel, know that I love you. And you're the best valentine I could ever have!

God, How I Love You

....

Kids sing about God's big, wide, deep love to the tune of "Pop, Goes the Weasel."

....

SCRIPTURE

Psalm 36

Sing It!

Your love is like a mountain

(Make a mountain shape with both arms)

Your love is like the ocean

(Make wave motions with hands)

Your love is big and wide and deep

(Motion with hands for each: big, wide, and deep)

God, how I love you!

(Place hands over heart.)

All throughout the world

(Sweep hands from left to right)

And all throughout the Bible

(Open hands like a book)

Your love is big and wide and deep

(Motion with hands for each: big, wide, and deep)

God, how I love you!

(Place hands over heart.)

Extra Special FACTOIDS

DID YOU KNOW...

1,317—That's how many companies in the U.S. produced chocolate and cocoa products in 2008. Those companies employed 38,369 people! The state with the most cocoa-creating companies? California, with 146, followed by Pennsylvania with 115.

DID YOU KNOW...

Legend has it that St. Valentine, the martyred saint from Ancient Rome after whom Valentine's Day is named, was killed for secretly marrying couples in defiance of an order of the Roman emperor. The emperor had forbidden marriage after Roman men began refusing to enlist to stay home with their wives.

Valentine's Day

True Love

The Experience

Find a retirement home in your community and schedule a time around Valentine's Day when your kids can visit and perform. Let the retirement home representative know this performance is especially for those who've lost a spouse.

Meet with kids beforehand to prepare. SAY: **Valentine's Day celebrates love and romance, but it can be a difficult day for those who are single, especially those people who've lost a husband or wife.**

Read aloud James 1:27.

Give kids card stock, markers, and stickers to make cards for widows and widowers in the retirement home. Then learn and practice a song about God's love that you can sing to your valentine recipients. For example, you might sing "Oh, the Deep, Deep Love of Jesus," or "Behold What Manner of Love."

Take up an offering to buy carnations; then deliver a flower and card to widows and widowers on Valentine's Day at the retirement home. Serenade them with the song you learned. Have kids show love by interviewing recipients, using the questions below as a guide.

- How do you like to show people love?
- What have you learned about love in your lifetime?
- In what ways have people shown you love?
- What do you think of when you hear the word *love*?

BEST
All Ages
FOR

Bring some Valentine's Day cheer to those who've lived— and loved—the longest.

SCRIPTURE

James 1:27

WHAT YOU'LL NEED

- Bible
- card stock
- markers
- stickers

JUST FOR FUN...

Attending a wedding for the first time, a little girl whispered to her mother, "Why is the bride dressed in white?"

"Because white is the color of happiness, and today is the happiest day of her life."

The child thought about this for a moment, then said, "So why is the groom wearing black?"

St. Patrick's Day

The wearin' o' the green

O n its surface, St. Patrick's Day seems to be all about good luck and mischievous leprechauns. But the real story behind this holiday is about a man who loved to share God's good news regardless of his circumstances. He even used shamrocks as a way to share his faith. As kids enjoy these St. Patrick's Day activities, they'll learn about the man behind the holiday—and about how God's blessings are greater than any luck a leprechaun could bring.

Devotion

St. Patrick's Shamrock

BEST Elementary FOR

Kids will learn about the Trinity— St. Patrick's way.

SCRIPTURE

Romans 8:15; John 3:16; John 20:21-22

WHAT YOU'LL NEED

- Bible
- 3 heart stickers per person
- picture of a shamrock

The Experience

SAY: **I'd like to tell you about a boy named Patrick. He was born in Great Britain, and his dad and grandfather both worked in a church. When Patrick was about 16, pirates captured him! The pirates took him to Ireland and sold him as a slave. Captured by pirates and sold into slavery— can you imagine? I'm guessing that Patrick's life didn't turn out the way he'd planned.**

ASK: **Tell us about a time things didn't go the way *you'd* planned.**

SAY: **After six years, Patrick escaped and decided he'd follow God. During the six years he'd lived as a slave, Patrick never lost faith. In fact, he prayed every day.**

ASK: **What do you pray about every day?**

SAY: **Even though his entire life changed, Patrick wasn't angry or hateful toward the people of Ireland. Instead, he wanted to teach them about God! One clever way he did that was by using things they were familiar with. Patrick wanted people to understand how God,**

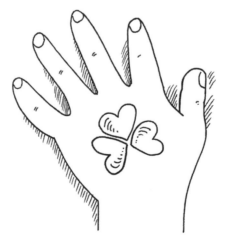

Jesus, and the Holy Spirit are all one.

Hold up a picture of a shamrock. Explain that a shamrock in Ireland would be as common as a blade of grass to us.

Read aloud Romans 8:15. Hand each child a heart sticker, and have kids place the sticker on the back of their hands. Explain that this sticker represents God, our Father.

Read aloud John 3:16. Hand each child a second heart sticker, and have kids place the second sticker next to the first one so the points of the hearts touch. Explain that the second sticker represents Jesus—God's incredible Son who came to earth to die for our sins.

Read aloud John 20:21-22. Hand each child a third sticker, and have kids place that sticker on the back of their hands so the points of all three stickers touch, creating a shamrock shape. Explain that the last sticker represents the Holy Spirit—the helper God gives to guide us.

SAY: **The shape on your hand is a lot like a shamrock—a plant people in Ireland see all the time!**

ASK: **What other things in nature remind you of God?**

SAY: **Patrick helped people understand God's great love and power through a simple plant.**

He helped them understand that even though God has three parts, he is one God. Point to the parts of a heart shamrock on kids' hands. **This represents God the Father, God the Son, and God the Holy Spirit. Now, every time you see a shamrock, *you* can be like Patrick and help people know more about God.**

Lucky Charms

Kids will make a lucky charm as they learn the difference between luck and blessings.

SCRIPTURE

Matthew 5:3-11

WHAT YOU'LL NEED

- Bibles
- 4 white cone-type coffee filters per child
- blue and yellow washable markers
- spray bottle with water
- newspaper or a tarp
- 11x17 construction paper
- cooling racks (used in baking)
- glue sticks
- black markers

The Experience

<u>SAY:</u> **When we think about St. Patrick's Day, we think about good luck.**

<u>ASK:</u> **What trinkets or items do people sometimes believe can bring good luck?**

<u>SAY:</u> **One symbol of luck associated with St. Patrick's Day is a four-leaf clover. Let's make some four-leaf clovers as we learn about luck.**

Have kids each color four coffee filters with blue and yellow washable markers, using more yellow than blue. Place the filters on newspaper or a tarp, and spray them with water. The colors will blend together. Then place the filters on a cooling rack to dry.

Form eight groups if possible, but keep at least two kids per group. If you can't make eight groups, then assign groups additional verses. Have groups each look up one verse of Matthew 5:3-11. Have groups read aloud their verses in order so everyone can hear all verses.

<u>ASK:</u> **Explain whether the situation in your verse sounds lucky.**

- **What's the difference between being blessed and being lucky?**

<u>SAY:</u> **Let's finish our four-leaf clovers. But rather than using them as a sign of good luck, let's use them to thank God for his blessings.**

Have kids glue the filters onto the construction paper in the shape of a four-leaf clover and use markers to draw a stem. Then have kids use the black markers to write one blessing on each coffee filter.

<u>SAY:</u> **The Bible doesn't have a lot to say about being lucky. But it has a lot to say about being blessed. This St. Patrick's Day, when you see something that points to good luck, remember that with God, we don't need luck. He loves us and gives us blessings every day— we just have to pay attention to see them.**

Game

Spread-the-word Tag

Kids will gather together in this St. Patrick's Day twist on the familiar game of Tag.

WHAT YOU'LL NEED

• large open space

The Experience

Gather kids in a large, open space—in a fellowship hall or a field. Choose one child to be the "Tagger." Have the rest of the kids stand at one end of your area. Explain that the Tagger is the young Patrick.

SAY: **Patrick stayed in Ireland to tell people about God. He used a shamrock to explain how God, Jesus, and the Holy Spirit are three, but part of one whole. The object of this game is for our Patrick to end up with the most people on his or her team before the game ends.** Explain that when you yell, "Go!" everyone must run from one side to the other without getting tagged. **If you** *do* **get tagged, link arms with Patrick...and keep tagging people! Ready? Go!**

After kids run back and forth five times, count how many haven't been tagged and how many the Tagger won over to his or her side.

ASK: **Tell about a time you were able to "catch" people for Jesus. Maybe you brought them to church or you helped them believe in Jesus.**

• **What's hard or easy about talking about your faith with others who might not know Jesus?**

• **Who's someone you can tell about Jesus this week?**

SAY: **Usually when we talk about St. Patrick's Day, we picture leprechauns and shamrocks. But St. Patrick's Day is really about celebrating a man named Patrick who helped people understand and love God. Like Patrick, we can lead people to God by taking them by the hand and telling them about what Jesus has done for us.**

Lost Gold Coins

Kids will look for the gold coin at the end of their rainbow snack—and learn how coins can show us how much God cares about us.

SCRIPTURE

Luke 15:8-10

WHAT YOU'LL NEED

- Bible
- solid-colored plastic cups
- vanilla wafer cookies
- cut-up strawberries
- banana slices
- green grapes, halved
- blueberries
- purple grapes, halved
- spoons

The Experience

SAY: **Around St. Patrick's Day, people often talk about leprechauns, rainbows, and hidden gold. Leprechauns are imaginary creatures who** *love* **their gold coins, which they hide in a pot at the end of a rainbow. Let's make a rainbow snack of our own to remind of us another kind of gold during St. Patrick's Day.**

Give each child a cup, a spoon, and a vanilla wafer cookie. Have kids put their cookies in the bottom of their cups and then use their spoons to scoop the different kinds of fruit into their cups. Kids might make rows of all the same fruit for a rainbow look, or they might mix them up.

As kids eat their snacks, SAY: **Right now, your "coin" is hidden. We need to find our missing coin! Let's hear about someone else who was looking for a coin.** Read Luke 15:8-10.

ASK: **Tell about a time you lost something.**

• **How is the way you felt about the item you lost like or unlike how God feels about you?**

SAY: **If you haven't already eaten your coin, find it, and hold it up.** Pause. **St. Patrick's Day is about a real man named Patrick who loved to tell people about Jesus. He understood that just like the woman and her lost coin, God wants everyone to be with him. Eat your coin and thank God that he wants to be your friend.**

The Dude in Green

A man is confused about why we celebrate St. Patrick's Day.

PROPS

- a cutout of a shamrock
- a box of Lucky Charms cereal

CAST

- Dude
- Girl

BEHIND THE SCENES

The simple setup is a blank stage. The Dude can be as green as you want, with a green shirt, green hat, any St. Patrick's Day accessories, and even green face paint. The girl could be wearing glasses and look like a little teacher.

Action!

➡ *The Dude enters the room, decked out in head-to-toe green. He's carrying a box of Lucky Charms cereal.*

DUDE

Yo! Kids! Don't you know it's almost St. Patrick's Day? *(Pause.)* If you know what color is usually seen on St. Patrick's Day, shout it out! *(Pause for kids to shout out answers.)* Yes! *Green!* You should all be wearing green...like me!

➡ *He reaches the stage, where the girl is standing.*

GIRL

St. Patrick's Day is *tomorrow.*

DUDE

Never too early to start celebrating, my wee bonny lass. *(To the audience)* Kids! Hold one hand up like this.

➡ *The Dude holds up his hand with his fingers spread apart—but with his middle and pointer finger touching, and his ring finger and pinky touching—leaving a "V" space in the middle.*

DUDE

It looks like a shamrock! Shamrock Slap some people around you by giving a high five with your hand like that! Woo!

➡ *Pause as kids Shamrock Slap.*

GIRL

Shamrock Slap? Really?

DUDE

You know it! What's your name, by the way?

GIRL

My name is Julie.

DUDE

Right. *(Pause.)* So, Jules, level with me. Where's your green?

GIRL

Do you even know why you're celebrating St. Patrick's Day?

DUDE

'Cause I get to eat Lucky Charms all day long, little Shamrock Shake.

GIRL

My name is Julie. And Lucky Charms don't have anything to do with St. Patrick's Day.

DUDE

Well, I like green. It brings out the color in my eyes.

GIRL

Do you know who St. Patrick was?

DUDE

Of course. *(Pause.)* He was a leprechaun, right?

GIRL

Patrick was a man who loved God—a lot!

DUDE

Whoa. That's heavy.

GIRL

No, here's the heavy part. When he was 16, pirates kidnapped him and made him a slave. To get through the bad times, he prayed. Actually, he prayed a lot. And God was with Patrick the entire time. Finally, he made it back home. Then, in a dream one night, Patrick heard God tell him to go back to Ireland to the people who'd kidnapped him to tell them about God.

DUDE

No way. Was he wearing green?

GIRL

You're missing the point.

DUDE

I've heard that before. So what happened to Pat?

GIRL

He went back and told the people all about God, using this.

➡ *She hands him a shamrock.*

DUDE

No way! A shamrock?

GIRL

Patrick explained that God is just like this shamrock—three in one: Father, Son, Holy Spirit.

DUDE

So, like, the shamrock has three petals, but it's all one leaf, right?

GIRL

Now you're catching on. Patrick taught thousands of people in Ireland about God. Not bad for a life's work.

DUDE

Wow. That's so cool. Can I still wear green, though?

GIRL

Of course! But just remember that Patrick was a great man of God—and the holiday isn't about a color.

DUDE

You got it—and I'm never gonna eat Lucky Charms the same way again.

➔ *Girl rolls her eyes and shrugs.*

St. Patrick's Hurrah

BEST
Preschool
FOR
....

A fun, singable melody about St. Patrick, sung to the tune of "When Johnny Comes Marching Home."

....

SCRIPTURE

Mark 16:15

Sing It!

St. Patrick went to Ireland, hur-rah, hur-rah!

(March in place.)

A shamrock in his holy hand, hur-rah, hur-rah!

(March in place; hold out right hand, palm up.)

The Holy Spirit, God, and Son

(March in place; put hands together as if in prayer)—

The shamrock he showed everyone

(March in place; move hands out, palms up, as if to "show everyone"),

And they all praised God when

St. Patrick came marching home.

(March in place.)

Extra Special
FACTOID

DID YOU KNOW...

A shamrock is a plant with heart-shaped leaves. The rare four-leaf clover is actually a mutated three-leaf clover, and its lobes are more rounded, not heart-shaped. The four-leaf clover is thought to be a lucky omen because it's so hard to find—with an estimated 10,000 three-leaf clovers occurring in nature for every one of the four-leaf variety.

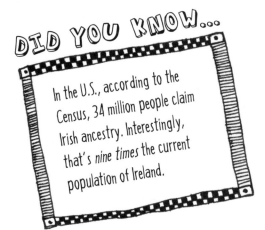

Beautiful Feet

BEST For All Ages

Kids will share the good news of Jesus by collecting shoes and socks for the needy.

Scripture

Isaiah 52:7

What You'll Need

- Bible
- paper
- pencils

The Experience

SAY: **Patrick had to walk a lot to tell the Irish people about God. I bet his feet got tired. And that reminds me of a verse.** Read Isaiah 52:7. **Patrick must've had beautiful feet, because he was a man who loved to share the good news. Let's follow Patrick. We're going to collect shoes and socks for people who can't afford them. We'll put notes in the footwear to share the good news, just like Patrick.**

Allow a few weeks for kids to collect new shoes and socks for a shoe drive, whether they do this independently or through a churchwide drive. Then have kids write notes that share the good news of Jesus, such as, "Jesus loves you!" Put the notes in the shoes, or tape them to sock packages. Then arrange a time for the kids and you to deliver the shoes to a local homeless shelter.

Extra Special FACTOIDS

DID YOU KNOW...

The color originally associated with St. Patrick was blue. In fact, the Order of St. Patrick's color, for the emblem or badge representing the Order, is "St. Patrick's Blue."

DID YOU KNOW...

In the U.S., according to the Census, 34 million people claim Irish ancestry. Interestingly, that's *nine times* the current population of Ireland.

Palm Sunday

Hosanna Hosanna

Less than a week before the crowds clamored for Jesus' crucifixion, they hailed him as their King. Jesus, the humble king, rode through the streets of Jerusalem on a donkey, just as prophecies had foretold. In amazement, the crowds spread their coats and palm branches on the road before Jesus and shouted his praises. Their excitement was growing so much that Matthew described the scene as an "uproar." As kids learn about this remarkable event, they'll discover how Jesus is worthy of their praise.

True Worship

Kids will offer worship to the greatest celebrity of all.

SCRIPTURE

Mark 11:1-11

WHAT YOU'LL NEED

- Bible
- green paper
- colored paper

The Experience

Open your Bible to Mark 11:1-11 and show kids the words.

SAY: **On Palm Sunday we remember when Jesus rode into Jerusalem on a donkey. The Bible says that huge crowds were excited and waiting for him as he entered the city.**

ASK: **When have you been part of a huge crowd? What was it like?**

SAY: **Let's see what it might've been like to be part of the crowd that followed Jesus on Palm Sunday.**

Form two groups. Give kids in one group each a green sheet of paper to represent the palms. Give kids in the other group each a colored sheet of paper to represent the coats. Then have kids spread out around the room. Stand in the center of the room.

Read Mark 11:8. SAY: **The people in the crowd laid palm branches and coats on the road as Jesus rode through the city. They did this to praise him and show him honor.** Have kids wave their green papers in the air and place the colored papers and green papers on the ground as they move toward the center of the room, surrounding you.

Read Mark 11:9-10. SAY: **The crowd surrounded Jesus. Then they shouted, "Praise God! Blessings on the one who comes in the name of the Lord." Let's shout, too!** Have kids shout "Praise God! Blessings on the one who comes in the name of the Lord." Then have kids sit.

ASK: **Tell about a celebrity you'd be super excited to see in person.**

• **How does the way you'd treat that celebrity compare to the way you treat Jesus each day?**

SAY: **People tend to worship celebrities, whether they're singers, actors, or athletes. But Jesus is the only one worthy of our worship, and we can worship him every day. We can worship Jesus by singing, praying, or serving him. Let's worship Jesus together with a praise prayer right now.**

Have kids form a circle. Ask each child to name something he or she loves or knows about Jesus and then give the person to the right a high five. Continue around the circle until everyone has shared. Then pray: **Dear Jesus, we love you and praise you. Thank you for** [name some of the things the kids said]**! Amen.** End by having a big round of applause for Jesus.

Donkey Glove

BEST
Upper Elementary
FOR

Jesus asked for a donkey—so kids will make him one!

SCRIPTURE

Matthew 21:1-3

WHAT YOU'LL NEED

- Bible
- 1 knit glove per child
- poly-fiber filling
- black yarn
- black felt
- scissors
- small black beads
- hot glue gun

The Experience

Read Matthew 21:1-3. <u>SAY:</u> **Jesus needs a donkey—let's make some for him.**

1. Give each child one glove and enough filling to stuff the fingers and palm of the glove.

2. Have kids turn the cuff of the glove to the inside and also tuck the thumb in approximately 1 inch, so the donkey's "nose" is shorter.

3. Have kids cut approximately eight 1½-inch lengths of yarn for the mane and three 3-inch lengths of yarn for the tail. Kids can work together to braid the tail and tie a knot on each end of the braid.

4. Fold the short yarn pieces in half and glue them in the folded cuff of the glove over the thumb.

5. Glue one end of the tail in the folded cuff of the glove opposite the thumb. Fray the yarn ends on the mane and the end of the tail.

6. Cut ear shapes from black felt. Crease the bottom and glue each ear about ¾-inch below the mane on either side of the glove, directly above the first finger.

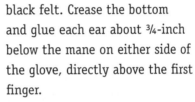

7. Glue small black beads as eyes on either side of the glove.

8. Help kids loop a 10- to 12-inch piece of yarn around the donkey's nose, tying it under the nose. Then kids will lay the long ends up over the donkey's back and tie them to form a bridle. Cut off excess yarn.

Palm Sunday

The Wave Parade

BEST
All Ages
FOR

With a ball and a passage from Mark, kids will have fun trying to keep up with this fast-moving game.

SCRIPTURE

Mark 11:8-10

WHAT YOU'LL NEED

• Bible
• ball

Extra Special
FACTOID

DID YOU KNOW...

There are over 2,500 species of palm trees! In ancient Roman times, the leaves were used as a reward for the early Olympic games. They were also used by early Christians to celebrate victory, and were laid on the ground as Jesus entered Jerusalem—hence the name "Palm Sunday."

The Experience

Read aloud the account of Palm Sunday from Mark 11:8-10.
<u>ASK:</u> **Tell about a time you were at a parade.**

<u>SAY:</u> **Sometimes you have to move to get a good view of what's happening at a parade. I imagine that's what happened to all the kids who were there when Jesus entered town on Palm Sunday. Let's see how quick you are at moving your feet when something moves by.**

Form a line so kids are side-by-side, with about 3 feet between each person. (If you have more than 10 kids, form two groups.) Explain that you'll roll a ball down the line—and the ball will represent Jesus passing by. <u>SAY:</u> **As soon as "Jesus" passes you, you'll run to the far end of the line and stand next to the last person in line—that way you're ready to see the ball (I mean, Jesus) going by again. Our entire line will move, one person at a time. Got it? Let's start with a practice round.**

Roll the ball *very* slowly, so kids get the hang of running to the end of the line and taking a new place as the ball passes them. Try a few more times, rolling the ball more quickly each time. Kids will most likely end up in a jumble, trying to get in line, but that's the point! Play several times, varying the speed of your roll.

<u>SAY:</u> **Palm Sunday was a big, noisy celebration...just like this was. Let's close with a celebration wave as Jesus passes by.** Roll the ball down the line, this time having kids cheer and wave as the ball goes by.

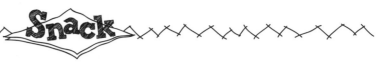

Palm Sunday Salad

BEST FOR All Ages

With lettuce palms and a ranch-dressing road, kids will enjoy a healthy snack to celebrate Palm Sunday.

SCRIPTURE

Matthew 21:5

ALLERGY ALERT See p. 7

WHAT YOU'LL NEED

- Bible
- paper plates
- baby carrots, cut in half
- baby tomatoes
- ranch dressing
- small-leaf lettuce or spinach leaves
- cheese slices
- forks

The Experience

Hand out the paper plates. SAY: **The very first Palm Sunday was a very exciting day. Imagine for a moment what it would be like to be in town when, all of a sudden, Jesus comes riding along the road.** Have kids make a road of ranch dressing down the center of their plates. **A crowd had gathered—a big crowd full of people excited to see Jesus. Let's use our carrots and tomatoes to create a crowd in our town.** Let

kids line their tomatoes and baby carrots on either side of the ranch-dressing road. (Kids should be able to stand the carrots on the flat end where they were cut.)

SAY: **The crowd waved their palm leaves to welcome Jesus into the city. As he arrived, they threw their leaves onto the road to create a path for him and to worship him.** Have kids place lettuce or spinach "palm leaves" along the ranch-dressing road. **They also threw down their coats to help make the path for Jesus.** Place cheese slices along the ranch-dressing road. **The crowd celebrated all day, and now we can celebrate with our very own Palm Sunday Salad!**

Distribute forks, and have kids mix up their salads and eat them as you discuss these questions.

ASK: **Why do you think the crowd was so excited to see Jesus?**

• **People in the crowd gave up their valuable coats in honor of Jesus. What would you give up in honor of him?**

Read Matthew 21:5. SAY: **When Jesus came through town, the people recognized him as king—and they treated him like one. When we worship Jesus and make sacrifices for him, we're treating him like our King, too.**

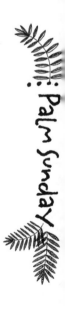

Palm Sunday

It's a Great Day to Sell Palm Fronds

BEST All Ages FOR

The life of a palm frond salesman changes dramatically when demand for palm fronds increases on a specific day.

SCRIPTURE

Matthew 21:1-11

PROPS

- a sign that reads, "Palm Fronds for Sale, 3 for $1.00"
- a table
- a basket or box of palm fronds (these can be construction paper cutouts, made to look like palm fronds)

CAST

- Marge
- Fred
- Man
- Woman
- Little Boy

BEHIND THE SCENES

The simple setup is a table with the sign taped to it. Fred is holding the basket or box of palm fronds as his wife Marge walks in.

 **Action!**

MARGE

Fred, we need to talk.

FRED

Uh-oh.

MARGE

I've been a good wife. A great wife, some might say. When you wanted to go into this business, I stuck up for you and said you were creative. Said you were unique. But Fred? Something's gotta give.

FRED

I know. It's been two years since I started selling the palm leaves. But I've got a good feeling!

MARGE

Two years, three months, 16 days to be exact. And how many leaves have you sold?

FRED

Well, just the one, but it was quite an important sale. I'm sure word is gonna spread.

➡ *She shoots him a look.*

FRED

I got a feeling about today, Marge. I just do. God wouldn't have told me to do this for no reason.

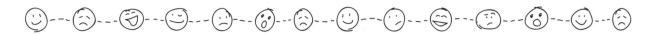

MARGE

I don't know...Let me know how it goes today.

➡ *Exits stage.*

Fred crosses the stage to where his sales cart is set up and starts calling out to people passing by.

FRED

Palm leaves! Get your palm leaves here! Palm leaves, just three for a dollar!

MAN

What a great idea! We can wave the palm leaves! You're a genius! I'll take three.

FRED

You will?

MAN

Of course! Great timing, man.

➡ *Fred is confused, but goes back to selling.*

FRED

Palm leaves! Get your palm leaves here! Palm leaves, just three for a dollar.

WOMAN

These are just what we need! Perfect! I'll take one for each of my 12 children. We can wave them when he comes by. These are the perfect way to welcome him!

FRED

Welcome who?

WOMAN

You're funny. Thanks for the leaves, sir! You're a genius!

FRED

Palm leaves! Get your palm leaves here! Palm leaves, just three for a dollar!

LITTLE BOY

I don't have much money, sir. Will this buy me a leaf? *(He holds out a coin.)*

FRED

(Takes the coin, and studies the little boy.) **Of course, son. Why is buying a palm leaf so important to you?**

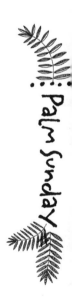

BOY

It's Jesus, sir. He's coming here. Today. We're going to wave the leaves and welcome him like a king. Because that's what he is. He's coming now! I have to go!

➡ *Fred looks out across the audience at an imaginary Jesus riding by. He starts on the left and pans to the right, and near the end he stops, almost surprised.*

FRED

He looked right me. And he smiled. The King of kings.

MAN

(Running up) We need more palm leaves! Hurry! We'll take all you have!

FRED

He looked right at me...

➡ *Marge re-enters.*

FRED

Marge! Look! I told you I had a feeling! Ha, ha!

MARGE

Fred, I...I can't believe it!

➡ *Hugs Fred while jumping up and down.*

Jesus Came to Town

BEST Preschool FOR

Celebrate with an easy-to-remember song that reminds little ones of when Jesus came to Jerusalem. Sing to the tune of "London Bridge."

SCRIPTURE

Matthew 11:1-11

Sing It!

Jesus came to town one day
(Right arm moving as if to say "Come here"),

Town one day, town one day.
(Left arm moving the same, then right arm again.)

Jesus came to town one day
(Right arm moving as if to say "Come here")—

He waved as he went by.
(Wave right hand.)

People waved their palms that day
(Wave right hand),

Palms that day, palms that day.
(Wave left hand, then right hand.)

People waved their palms that day
(Wave right hand)—

They waved as he went by.
(Wave both hands.)

DID YOU KNOW...

Certain types of palm trees grow fruit. Among them, the Guadelupe Palm, the Chilean Wine Palm, and the Jelly Palm, which is native to Brazil and used for, you guessed it, jellies and jams.

DID YOU KNOW...

On Palm Sunday in England, some churches hand out small buns with an image of a lamb to congregation members. The buns are called pax cakes. ("Pax" is Latin for "Peace.")

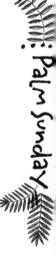

Palm Sunday

Victory Palms

Kids will make posters to help hospital patients keep a positive mindset.

SCRIPTURE

Romans 8:35-37

WHAT YOU'LL NEED

- Bible
- scissors
- paper
- art supplies such as markers, crayons, colored pencils, and glitter glue
- fake palm branches (available at craft stores)
- glue
- poster board
- clear vinyl adhesive paper

The Experience

Contact a local hospital and ask for permission to hang posters in waiting areas or common rooms where patients can see them. Once you have permission, get your kids together to create the posters.

SAY: **In Roman times, palm branches were symbols of triumph and winning, both in games and military successes. When Jesus rode into Jerusalem, the Jewish people honored him by lining the road with palm branches because they expected him to bring victory over the Roman rulers. Today when we think of winning, we don't usually think of palm leaves.**

ASK: **What things symbolize winning today?**

Have kids create pictures of trophies, crowns, medals, or other symbols of victory by drawing them with markers, crayons, colored pencils, or glitter glue. Then have kids make a victory collage by gluing the cutouts onto a poster board.

Have kids spell out the word *victory* with fake palm branches and glue it to the poster. Provide markers so kids can add other written words of encouragement and perseverance. Consider using the following Scriptures that talk about winning and triumph: Deuteronomy 20:4; 1 Corinthians 15:57; or James 1:12. When the posters are complete, laminate them with clear vinyl adhesive paper.

Read Romans 8:35-37. SAY: **There are people in our community who are threatened with death or injury, and they might feel like they're separated from Jesus' love. Let's give these posters to a local hospital to help patients there know that no matter what, victory is theirs with Jesus!**

Have kids hold their posters and take turns praying for strength and courage for the people who'll see the posters. Then take them to the hospital and display them.

REBIRTH

EASTER

D arkness consumed the earth. Earthquakes shattered rocks. Women wept. And then, after Jesus' friends placed him in the tomb, there was silence. After three days, though, there was confusion followed by glorious rejoicing as Jesus' followers found his empty tomb and learned that he'd come back to life. When kids celebrate Jesus' resurrection, they see that thanks to his victory over death we can have new life in Jesus.

51

Devotion

WASHED AWAY

BEST
All Ages
FOR

Kids will see their sins vanish as Jesus conquers death!

SCRIPTURE

1 Corinthians 15:54-57

WHAT YOU'LL NEED

• Bible
• tissues
• washable markers
• cups
• lukewarm water
• dish soap
• plastic bags

The Experience

Give each child a tissue, and have kids write or draw several things they've done wrong on the tissues. Younger kids can just make marks on the tissue to represent wrong things.

SAY: **Jesus died on the cross to forgive us for everything we've ever done wrong. His friends and family thought the story ended** there with his death. **Write the word** *death* **on top of all your sins.** Younger kids can just scribble all over their marks.

Give each child a cup with a small amount of dish soap and some lukewarm water. Have kids place the cup on top of a plastic bag to catch any drips. Then have them place their tissues into the cups and swirl them around as you read 1 Corinthians 15:54-57. SAY: **But Jesus' story didn't end with sin and death. He won! Lift your tissues out of the water and see what happened to your sin and death.** Allow time for kids to see that their tissues have come completely clean.

ASK: **How does this experience remind you of Jesus' forgiveness?**

• **What's one thing you can tell others that Easter means to you?**

SAY: **At Easter, we know that Jesus died for our sins so we can be forgiven. And we celebrate Jesus' winning over death because we know he beat our sins once and for all. And best of all, he wants us to live with him in heaven forever.**

STONES CRY OUT

BEST
Elementary
FOR

Kids create keepsake rocks to remind them of what Jesus did for us.

SCRIPTURE

Luke 19:39-40; Luke 22:39-41; Matthew 27:50-51; Luke 23:53; Luke 24:2-3

WHAT YOU'LL NEED

- Bible
- small rocks of various shapes, 5 per child
- fine-tipped permanent markers
- paper lunch bags
- stickers

The Experience

Ask kids to tell about interesting rocks or rock formations they've seen. <u>SAY:</u> **Stones and rocks are mentioned more than 400 times in the Bible. People used them to build altars to remember what God had done. Jesus told stories about stones. Stones were part of the landscape at the end of Jesus' life, too. Today we're going to make a rock collection to help us remember the story of Jesus' death and resurrection.**

Give each child five rocks and a permanent marker. <u>SAY:</u> **On the Sunday before he died, Jesus rode into Jerusalem. The people waved palm branches and praised him. And Jesus said something about rocks. Let's see what he said.** Read Luke 19:39-40. Have kids draw a palm branch on a rock to represent the crowd's praise.

<u>ASK:</u> **What are some ways you praise Jesus?**

<u>SAY:</u> **On the night**

before he died, Jesus prayed in the Garden of Gethsemane. The Bible uses a rock as a measurement of where Jesus went to pray. Read Luke 22:39-41. Invite kids to draw a flower to represent the garden on one of the rocks.

<u>ASK:</u> **What do you need to pray about?** (Let kids answer silently or to the group.)

<u>SAY:</u> **When Jesus was on the cross, something happened to the rocks nearby.** Read Matthew 27:50-51. Have kids draw a lightning bolt on one rock to represent the stones splitting.

<u>ASK:</u> **How have you seen God's power in your life?**

<u>SAY:</u> **After Jesus died, a man named Joseph took Jesus' body from the cross and laid it in a tomb.** Read Luke 23:53. Invite kids to draw a cross on one of the rocks.

<u>ASK:</u> **Tell about something that makes you sad.**

<u>SAY:</u> **The reason people realized Jesus was alive had to do with a rock.** Read Luke 24:2-3. Have kids draw an arrow on one of the rocks to show that it rolled aside.

<u>ASK:</u> **Tell about a time you celebrated something.**

<u>SAY:</u> **The events of Easter start out sad; but in the end we see God's power, and we have reason to celebrate! Whenever you look at your rock collection, remember to praise Jesus for his power over death. Now let's decorate a place where you can keep your rocks.** Let kids use the markers and stickers to decorate their paper bags and then place their rocks inside.

EASTER

SLIDING STONE

BEST Elementary FOR

Kids will see the stone roll away in this exciting diorama.

SCRIPTURE

Matthew 28:2-4

WHAT YOU'LL NEED

- Bible
- small empty boxes
- scissors
- black or gray card stock
- gray and white craft paints
- paintbrushes
- clear tape
- wooden craft sticks
- black construction paper
- fake grass
- pebbles
- hot glue gun
- yellow cellophane or tissue paper

The Experience

Read Matthew 28:2-4. <u>SAY:</u> **It must've been quite a sight to see the stone rolled away and the tomb empty! Let's make a diorama—or a miniature scene—to see what it might've looked like.**

1. Have kids cut a piece of black or gray card stock the width and height of the inside of the box. Then have kids rough up the card stock by crumpling and uncrumpling it. They can dab gray and white paint on the

> *Tip* Want to go all out? Use black foam core rather than card stock to create your tomb wall and stone. Add texture by hammering the foam core. In addition to the pebbles and grass, use sand and twigs to make the front of the tomb really pop.

crumpled card stock to make the surface look like a stone wall.

2. Cut out a circle shape approximately 2½ inches in diameter from the bottom center of the card stock, and set it aside. This shape will be the stone, and the hole will be the opening of the tomb.

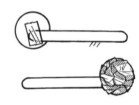

3. Have kids tape the edges and bottom of the stone wall inside the box, approximately centered.

back ↑

4. Have kids tape one end of a wooden craft stick to the lower part of the backside of the stone shape. Then have kids paint the front side of the craft stick to match the stone.

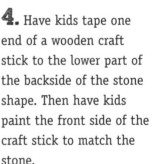

5. Just in front of the stone wall, help kids cut a small vertical slit approximately ½-inch long and close to the box bottom. From the inside of the box, slip the empty end of the craft stick through the slit and then align the stone with the tomb opening. The craft stick should extend out of the side of the box.

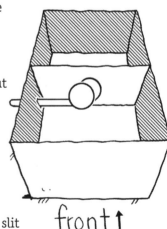

front ↑↑

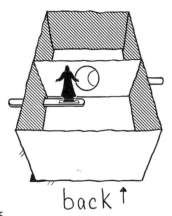

back ↑

6. Using the pattern to the right, have each child cut a figure of Jesus out of black paper. Have kids fold along the line and tape a craft stick to the bottom of the fold. Help kids cut a horizontal slit close to the bottom of the box about an inch behind the stone wall. Slide the stick through the slit from the inside so that Jesus lines up with the tomb opening.

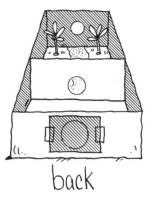

7. Have kids use the fake grass and pebbles to create a scene in the front half of the box. Help hot glue everything in place.

8. Help kids cut a 3-inch hole in the back of the box, behind the tomb opening. Kids can use tape to cover the hole with yellow cellophane or tissue paper. In the front end of the box, help kids cut a viewing hole approximately 1½-inches in diameter. Give kids tape to cover the top of the front part of the box with yellow cellophane or tissue paper, and have them cover the top of the back part with black construction paper.

9. Have kids stand under a light and tell the Easter story as they reenact it with their dioramas. They should start with both craft sticks pulled all the way to the edge. As they talk about how Jesus was buried in the tomb, they can slide him forward so he can be seen. Then they can slide the stone to cover the tomb entrance. When they tell about Easter morning, have them slide Jesus to the side and then pull back the stone to reveal the empty, shining tomb!

back   front

EASTER

Game

A COMMON THREAD

BEST
Elementary
FOR

Kids discover a common thread that shows we're all connected to Jesus' sacrifice.

SCRIPTURE

Mark 16:1-7

WHAT YOU'LL NEED

• Bible
• ball of yarn
• cross

Extra Special
FACTOID

DID YOU KNOW...

The all-time favorite Easter treat is, of course, the bountifully flavored jelly bean. Jelly Belly's Very Cherry jelly bean was the company's most popular flavor until 1998 when it was dethroned by Buttered Popcorn. Very Cherry regained the title in 2003, but only by a slim margin of 8 million beans.

The Experience

Have kids form a big circle. Keeping the cross hidden from view, hold up the ball of yarn and SAY: **Let's see how tangled up we can get! We have 60 seconds. I'll hold onto this end of the yarn, and I'll throw the ball to someone else in the circle. Once you get it, hang onto the yarn at the point you caught it, and toss the ball to someone else. The only rule is that you can't hand the ball of yarn to the person next to you. One minute. Ready? Go!**

While kids are busy tossing the yarn, tie your end of the yarn to the cross. When time is up, say to the person holding the ball:

• **Talk about a time someone did something amazing for you that made you feel really special.**

After the child has shared, have him or her stand and carefully roll the yarn back to the person who's holding it next.

Continue with the same question for each person (even when kids go twice), until the yarn ball is back to you.

Hold up the cross that's now attached to the yarn and SAY: **Through all of us there is a common thread. Just as you shared about people in your lives doing amazing things for you, Jesus did something amazing for all of us 2,000 years ago on a cross. And a most amazing thing happened three days later.**

Read Mark 16:1-7.

ASK: **What amazes you about Jesus?**

• **Turn to the person next to you and find a "common thread" between you—something you both find amazing about Jesus.**

SAY: **Jesus gave his life for each of you. It's the one thing that ties us back to him; and when we tell others about how amazing Jesus is, it's like throwing a ball of yarn to them. It connects you, just as you're connected to Jesus!**

GOOD NEWS BOUQUET

 BEST For All Ages

As kids create these edible bouquets, they'll learn that they're alive with Jesus!

SCRIPTURE

Romans 6:7-10

 ALLERGY ALERT *See p. 7*

WHAT YOU'LL NEED

- Bible
- clear plastic cups
- Chex Mix
- marshmallows
- kabob skewers
- bowls
- white frosting
- plastic knives
- colored sprinkles or confectionary confetti
- green construction paper
- scissors
- tape

The Experience

SAY: **Easter is a time when we remember life. Trees sprout leaves, animals that were hibernating come out, and most importantly, Jesus came back to life!**

ASK: **Name things that are alive. How do you know those things are alive?**

SAY: **One thing that dies every winter but comes back to life in the spring is a flower. Let's make some edible flowers.** Set out the ingredients. Place frosting, confetti, and sprinkles in bowls.

Help kids fill the clear plastic cups with Chex Mix. Then have kids stick a marshmallow on a kabob skewer and then use a plastic knife to spread frosting on the marshmallow. Help younger children

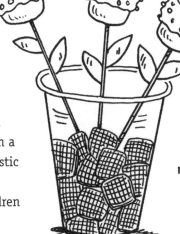

with the skewer and frosting. Then let kids roll the frosted marshmallow in the sprinkles or confetti, creating the flower and stem. Have kids place the flower in the cup and make two more like it.

Give kids green construction paper and have them cut leaves and tape them to the skewer stems. For younger kids, simply tear small scraps of green paper and help kids tape them onto the stems.

Let kids enjoy their snack as you read Romans 6:7-10.

SAY: **Our flower can remind us that Jesus died on the cross for our sins and came back to life. Because Jesus came back to life, we can have a new life, too. All the sins we're tempted by don't have any power over us, thanks to Jesus.**

ASK: **How can you tell if someone is alive in Jesus?**

SAY: **Think about some of the bad things in your life that seem to have power over you. For example, maybe it's hard for you not to be mean to your brother. Or maybe you use naughty words. Say a silent prayer that Jesus will help you see how he can help you with all those things.**

Allow a few moments and then PRAY: **Dear God, thank you for beating our sins, not just so you could forgive us, but also so you could help us do the right thing. In Jesus' name, amen.**

 EASTER

STAINED GLASS CROSS COOKIES

BEST
Elementary
FOR

*Kids will journey to the cross
with this sweet treat.*

SCRIPTURE

Acts 13:29-31

WHAT YOU'LL NEED

- Bible
- red, hard candies, such as Jolly Ranchers or Life Savers
- sandwich bags
- rolling pins, hammers, or meat mallets
- cookie sheets
- parchment paper
- Pillsbury sugar cookie dough, chilled
- flour
- cross cookie cutters in varying sizes
- knife
- cooling racks
- spatula
- oven
- oven mitt

The Experience

Have kids wash their hands. SAY: **The cross is a very important symbol for us. Jesus died on the cross, stained with his blood, so our sins could be forgiven. Let's roll out our cookie dough and cut crosses to remind us of what Jesus did for us. As you cut your cross, think about things you've done wrong. Those are the things Jesus died to forgive.**

Preheat an oven to 350°F. Coat the sides of the cookie dough with 2 tablespoons of the flour. Roll out dough on a clean, flat surface until ⅛-inch thick, using additional flour as needed to prevent sticking. Have kids cut out the dough with floured, large cross-shaped cookie cutters. With smaller cross cookie cutters or butter knives, have kids cut out the center of the cookie, leaving

about ½-inch frame. Line cookie sheets with parchment paper and place the cookies on it.

SAY: **Let's hammer some red candy to remind us how Jesus was nailed to the cross. As you crush your candy, ask Jesus to forgive you for the things you've done wrong.** Give kids three or four pieces of red, hard candy, and have them crush the candy in a sandwich bag with rolling pins, hammers, or meat mallets. Help as needed.

SAY: **Let's put our crushed candies into the crosses to remind us of Jesus' blood Jesus. As you put your candy into your cross, thank Jesus for what he did for you.** Have fill the cookie cutouts with the crushed candy, making sure candy touches the edge of the cookie. Avoid mounding the candy in tall heaps.

SAY: **Now we'll put our cookies in the oven to remind us that Jesus went into a tomb. Smell the sweetness of the baking cookies and praise Jesus for his sweet love for you.** Bake the cookies for five to nine minutes or until the edges of the cookies are light golden brown and the candy is melted. Cool for a few minutes on cookie sheets until candy is hardened. Place cookies on cooling racks. Cool for about 15 minutes. Repeat with remaining dough and candy.

Read Acts 13:29-31. SAY: **Even though Jesus died on the cross and was buried in a tomb, he came back to life. That's what we celebrate on Easter! Let's eat our cookies to remind us that the tomb is empty and our sins are gone!**

Enjoy the cookies with your kids as you discuss these questions:

ASK: **What were some things you talked to Jesus about as you made these cookies?**

• **What will you do this week to celebrate that Jesus lives?**

THE BOX OF STONES

BEST
Upper Elementary
FOR

*An impactful skit that'll turn kids'
hearts toward Jesus.*

SCRIPTURE

Romans 6:8-9

PROPS

- a cardboard box filled with stones for each character.
- 10 stones, each labeled: "disobedient to parents," "swearing," "cheating on a math test," "shoplifting," "cheating," "making fun of people," "telling a big lie," "hatred," "complaining," and "lying"
- a card table
- 2 chairs
- a large cross
- a small stone for each audience member
- Joe Strock's *Surrender* CD (available on iTunes)
- "Come to Jesus" from Chris Rice's *Run the Earth, Watch the Sky* CD (available on iTunes)
- CD player

CAST

- Main child character
- Three child "friends," two male and one female
- Therapist (adult female, wears suit)
- Jesus (wears a white robe and a crown of thorns)
- Adult dressed in dark clothing
- Narrator (adult)

BEHIND THE SCENES

The therapist's office is set up with the table and chairs on the left hand side of the stage. The large cross is set up on the opposite side.

Give a small stone to each person in the audience.

Action!

→ *The Main Character enters from stage right, slowly moving toward center stage during the first paragraph. He struggles underneath a heavy load—a large, heavy cardboard box filled with stones.*

MAIN CHARACTER

I'm not exactly sure where it came from... this box of stones. It seems like I've been carrying it around all my life. It didn't used to be this heavy. It's sort of strange, but the older I get, the heavier it becomes. *(Looks tired; droops shoulders.)* **And as each day goes by, more and more stones get in my box.** *(Sets box on the floor and sits beside it.)*
I can barely remember finding the first stone. I think I was around 4 years old. I lied to my parents about breaking a vase. It was no big deal...but after I lied, that's when I noticed this box with a single stone inside. I pulled out the stone...

→ *The Main Character reaches in the box and searches through different stones, not finding it at first. He finds it and continues.*

MAIN CHARACTER

Yeah, here it is. The first stone. I pulled it out of the box...It was filthy. *(Wipes stone on jeans.)* **It had the word "lying" on**

EASTER

59

it. I just tossed it back in the box. *(Puts it back in the box.)* **No big deal...after all, it was just a little lie.**

→ *The Main Character pauses for a brief second. He shakes his head.*

MAIN CHARACTER

Yeah, right. It was no big deal...so why did I feel so bad? Why did I feel that no one could ever love me?

→ *The Main Character pauses again, looking into the box.*

MAIN CHARACTER

But now I have so many of these stones. *(Reaches in and pulls out a stone.)* **This one: "disobedient to parents"...so what? All they ever do is gripe at me anyway.** *(Puts the stone in the box and pulls out another.)* **"Swearing"...It's really tough to keep from letting a bad word slip out every now and then.** *(Pulls stones out faster and reads them.)* **Cheating on a math test, shoplifting, cheating again, making fun of people, telling a big lie, hatred, complaining, lying again.**

→ *The Main Character hangs his head in desperation. Then he puts the stones back in the box.*

MAIN CHARACTER

Before I knew it, I was carrying around this heavy box of stones. *(Slowly struggles to lift the box again.)* **Each stone is a reminder of filth in my life...each pound...the heaviness of sin in my life. I feel so bad. Why have I done all these things? Could anyone ever love me enough to forgive me?**

→ *The Main Character bows his head, and as he does, the track "He Is All You Need" begins to play.*

MAIN CHARACTER

I'm afraid to talk to my parents about all my stones. I know they'd really be disappointed in me. I tried talking to a friend about it.

→ *Friend #1 enters from stage right.*

MAIN CHARACTER

He took a stone out of the box. *(Friend #1 sets down his box and takes a stone from the Main Character's box. Friend #1 smiles as he looks at it.)* **He said, "What are you worried about? It's just a little sin!" Then he put the stone back in the box.** *(Friend #1 exits with his box stage left.)*

→ *Friend #2 enters from stage right.*

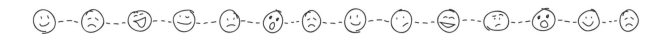

MAIN CHARACTER

Another friend was so shocked by what she read on the stones that she put them back in the box...looked at me with disgust...and walked away. *(Friend #2 sets down her box, peeks into the Main Character's box, looks shocked, picks up her own box, walks away, and exits stage left.)*

➡ *Friend #3 enters from stage right.*

MAIN CHARACTER

A close friend even helped me carry the box of stones around...but over time, it got too heavy and wore him down, too.** *(Friend #3 tries to carry the Main Character's box and his own box...eventually stumbles and lets go. Looks apologetic as he exits stage left with his box.)*

MAIN CHARACTER

It's okay; he had his own box of stones to carry. It was nice of him to help...but it was just too much weight to carry.

➡ *The Counselor enters from stage left and sets her box on the table. Main Character carries his box and joins the Counselor at the table.*

MAIN CHARACTER

Somebody told me I should see a counselor. That was okay...for a while. I would go into her office and empty the box of stones onto the table. *(Empties box of stones onto the table.)* **We talked about the stones...and believe me, that wasn't easy.** *(Both look at the stones as though analyzing them.)* **After looking through my stones, she told me it wasn't my fault. I was a victim. It was everyone else's fault. It felt good to talk about it, but after every session I'd pack the stones back in my box and drag them home.**

➡ *The Main Character places his box on floor and drags it to center stage. The Counselor exits left with her box.*

MAIN CHARACTER

I wish someone could help me. I'm so tired of stumbling under this load. I want some help! I want some relief! I want someone to love me and forgive me. *(Bows head with shoulders drooped and hand to forehead.)*

➡ *Song segment: Play "How Could You Say No?" by Joe Strock as Jesus enters from stage left and slowly walks to the Main Character. Jesus places his hand on the Main Character's shoulder, takes the box of stones, and slowly walks to the cross. Jesus empties the stones one by one at the foot of the cross, takes his place on the cross, and dies. Main Character and the person dressed in dark clothing take Jesus off the cross and slowly carry him as they exit stage right. The Narrator enters from stage left.*

NARRATOR

Behold, the Lamb of God, who takes away the sin of the world. God made Jesus—who knew no sin—to become sin that we might be made right with God. Jesus was wounded for all our sins. He was bruised for all the things we've done wrong. And by his punishment, we are healed.

➡ *This next segment is directed to the audience.*

NARRATOR

You've been holding a stone that represents sin in your life. In a moment, you'll have time to give it to Jesus and lay it at the foot of the cross. You'll take nothing away. The weight of your sin can be taken away by Jesus only. Because of our Savior's death on the cross and resurrection from the dead, you are free!

➡ *As children lay their stones at the cross and return to their seats, play "The Cross" by Joe Strock. After the last person is seated, darken the room and then play "Come to Jesus" by Chris Rice.*

The Main Character slowly enters and kneels at the cross. On the third chorus, turn on the stage lights as Jesus enters in a white robe. Jesus walks over to the cross, places his hand on the Main Character's shoulder, and whispers in his ear. The Main Character is startled as he stands up and steps back from Jesus. Jesus opens his arms. They embrace and exit arm in arm.

I'M THE LIFE, THE TRUTH, THE WAY

BEST Preschool FOR ....

Celebrate Easter with easy-to-learn lyrics, set to the tune of the "A, B, C Song."

....

SCRIPTURE

Galatians 1:4

Sing It!

Jesus came to earth to say

(Touch a finger to each palm; then cup hands around mouth as if telling),

"I'm the life, the truth, the way."

(Right thumb up, left thumb up, raise both hands up.)

Gave his life for you and me

(Point to others and then to self)—

Gave his life to set us free.

(Hands over face; then open them on "free.")

Jesus came to earth to say

(Touch a finger to each palm; then cup hands around mouth as if telling),

"I'm the life, the truth, the way."

(Right thumb up, left thumb up, raise both hands up.)

CHURCH SIGNS SEEN ON EASTER

Easter:
More Than Something to Dye For

Our Church:
Now Open Between Easter and Christmas!

Lent:
Spring Training for Christians
Easter:
OPENING DAY.

Jesus Paid the Price:
You Get to Keep the Change

EASTER

 BEST For All Ages

FOOD TO SPARE

Jesus told Peter, "Feed my lambs"—so kids will do just that in an Easter jelly bean drive.

SCRIPTURE

John 21:4-6, 12-13, 15-17

WHAT YOU'LL NEED

- Bible
- small, clean plastic jars
- jelly beans
- colorful paper
- hole punch
- markers
- ribbons

The Experience

In the weeks leading up to this project, collect small, clean jars and remove labels.

Gather your kids and SAY: **After Jesus came back to life, he appeared to his disciples. He made sure they had plenty of food to eat.**

ASK: **Tell about a time you were really hungry.**

Read John 21:4-6, 12-13. SAY: **Then Jesus told Peter how to show that he really loved Jesus.** Read John 21:15-17.

ASK: **Tell about a time you shared food with someone.**

SAY: **There are people in our town who are hungry. And we can show Jesus' love by feeding his lambs a special Easter treat—jelly beans!**

Have kids fill the jars with jelly beans and write notes or poems on colorful paper. Punch a hole in the corner of each card and string a piece of ribbon through the hole. Tie one note around each jar just underneath the lid. Give the goodies to a local food pantry to be distributed along with Easter food baskets, or have kids take them home to give to neighbors as an Easter outreach.

 Extra Special FACTOID

DID YOU KNOW...

Within the Catholic church, pretzels were once regarded as having religious significance. The traditional pretzel's "folded arms" resembled a person in prayer. Catholics could eat pretzels during Lent (the period between Ash Wednesday and Easter when Catholics observe fasting and penitence). During Lent, Catholics abstain from eating meat on Fridays, so pretzels made of flour and water offered a tasty alternative. Pretzels were often hidden on Easter for children to find.

EARTH DAY

When God created the world, he told people to take part in caring for it. Genesis 1:28 tells us to rule over the earth. Although Earth Day doesn't have roots in Christianity, we can celebrate this day as people who love God and want to fulfill his call to care for his creation. These activities will help kids understand why and how we can take care of God's earth.

HANDLE WITH CARE

 BEST Elementary FOR

Kids practice carefully caring for God's creation.

SCRIPTURE

Genesis 1:28-30

WHAT YOU'LL NEED

- Bible
- an egg, washed in soapy water and then treated with hand sanitizer prior to use
- paper towels

The Experience

SAY: **The Bible tells us God made the entire world—every rock, tree, giraffe, and dung beetle.**

ASK: **How would you describe the world God made?**

SAY: **After God made the earth, he gave people a *really* important job. Let's see what that was.** Read aloud Genesis 1:28-30.

ASK: **Explain whether you still think that's our job today.**

- **How do people do that job today?**

Hold up the egg. SAY: **Let's pretend that this egg is the** [*use words kids said to describe the world*] **world God made. And it's up to us to take care of it.**

Have kids stand in a circle. Demonstrate how to hold the egg one foot above the hand of the person to your left. Drop the egg into that person's open palm. Pass the egg carefully around the circle, dropping it into each person's hand. (It's okay if the egg breaks—you'll make an even stronger point! Just use paper towels to clean it up.) Set the egg aside when it returns.

ASK: **What were you feeling as you passed the egg?**

- **How did those feelings impact the way you handled the egg?**
- **How is this experience like or unlike taking care of the earth God gave us?**

SAY: **On Earth Day, we hear a lot about taking care of the world. When we love God, we can show our love for him on Earth Day by taking care of what he created. So every time you recycle, pick up trash, or turn off a light, you're doing a job God gave especially to you.**

Craft

SALVAGE AND RECYCLE

*Clean up your resource
room and recycle leftovers
with this easy craft.*

SCRIPTURE

2 Corinthians 5:17

WHAT YOU'LL NEED

- Bible
- green paper plates
- blue modeling dough
- various recyclables and extra
  craft supplies, including toilet
  paper rolls, paper towel rolls,
  egg cartons, old bolts and
  screws, colored craft sticks,
  pompom balls, chenille wires,
  and more
- permanent markers

The Experience

SAY: **This week we're celebrating Earth Day, a day set aside for appreciating and caring for the earth. One thing we can do to care for the earth is recycle. That helps make the earth's resources last longer. Recycling goes back pretty far in history; in fact, the Bible says Jesus recycled us!** Read 2 Corinthians 5:17.

ASK: **What do you think are some old things Jesus gets rid of in us?**

- **How has Jesus transformed you into something amazing?**

SAY: **Today we're going to recycle and repurpose old things to make a new creation.** Have kids roll the modeling dough into a ball and press it flat onto the center of the plate. Then kids can create their salvage sculptures by arranging supplies into the modeling dough base. Have kids write, "The old life is gone; a new life has begun!" on their plates.

SAY: **This Earth Day, remember to care for the earth the way Jesus cares for each of us—by recycling the old into something creative and new!**

CREATION SCULPTURES

Kids are the sculptures in this creatively interactive game.

SCRIPTURE

Genesis 2:9-12, 15

WHAT YOU'LL NEED

• Bible

The Experience

SAY: **God created an entire world full of things—like trees, water, and stones—that we use to make** *other* **things that help us live. Listen.** Read Genesis 2:9-12.

ASK: **What kinds of things do people make with trees, water, or stones?**

SAY: **Today, we're using something else God made to create—us! Let's play Creation Sculptures.**

Have kids sit in a circle, leaving a good-sized space in the middle. Ask three children to stand in the center of the circle and, whispering so the rest of the circle can't hear, have them discuss a position they can freeze in that shows something in God's creation. For example, one child might crouch down on all fours, and

another might freeze behind that person with an arm extended to look like the trunk of an elephant. Encourage kids to think creatively and be willing to laugh and have fun with it.

Once the three children have decided and posed, have the other kids in the circle call out what part of creation they think the sculpture represents. Once someone guesses correctly, read Genesis 2:15. Then have kids call out different ways to protect or take care of the part of creation that the Creation Sculpture represented. Continue playing as time allows so each child has a chance to pose in a Creation Sculpture.

ASK: **What's one of your favorite things in all of God's creation?**

• **Talk about a time when you saw God's creation treated poorly.**

• **What can you do to protect and take care of what God made?**

SAY: **Earth Day is a special day to celebrate everything God made. On Earth Day, we stop to appreciate God's creations and learn ways to protect and keep those things safe. We can celebrate Earth Day by picking up trash, recycling rather than throwing away, or planting a tree as we remember that God created everything.**

SEVEN DAYS TO PRAISE

BEST All Ages FOR

Kids gobble up goodies as they praise God for his amazing creation.

SCRIPTURE

Psalm 148:3-5; Genesis 1:1–2:4a

ALLERGY ALERT *See p. 7*

WHAT YOU'LL NEED

- Bible
- white paper place mats
- markers
- light and dark colored sprinkles
- clear plastic cups
- milk and chocolate syrup
- spoons
- fruit pieces
- oranges, sliced
- cheese, cut in circles
- fish-shaped crackers
- animal crackers
- marshmallows

The Experience

SAY: **Earth Day is about God's amazing creation.** Read Psalm 148:3-5. **God's creation praises him—even the things that can't move or talk. And we can praise him for his creation, too. Let's make a snack to explore some of the things God created. But first, draw seven boxes on your place mats.** Distribute place mats and markers, and allow time for kids to draw boxes.

SAY: **On the first day of Creation, God separated light and darkness.** Spoon some sprinkles onto the first box on their place mats. **Separate your light and dark sprinkles as you share something with your neighbor that you love about the daylight or darkness.**

SAY: **Next, God separated the water and the sky. A little chocolate milk can help us think through what God did.** Distribute glasses of milk, and then add chocolate syrup.

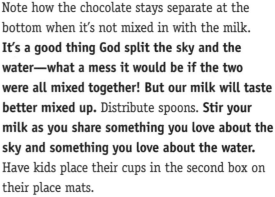

Note how the chocolate stays separate at the bottom when it's not mixed in with the milk. **It's a good thing God split the sky and the water—what a mess it would be if the two were all mixed together! But our milk will taste better mixed up.** Distribute spoons. **Stir your milk as you share something you love about the sky and something you love about the water.** Have kids place their cups in the second box on their place mats.

SAY: **Then God made the land and the seas. And on the land, he created plants and trees. That includes fruit that grows on plants and trees! Let's put some fruit pieces in our next box as we praise God for our favorite kind of fruit or vegetable.** Distribute the fruit.

SAY: **Next, God created the sun, moon, and stars. Let's put an orange-slice sun and a cheese moon in our fourth box. Then share one thing you love about the things God made to light up the sky.** Distribute orange slices and cheese circles.

SAY: **Then God filled the sky with birds and the waters with fish. Let's get a few fish for our fifth box as you tell about your favorite birds and fish.** Distribute fish-shaped crackers.

SAY: **Next, God put animals and people on the land. As you choose a couple of animal crackers for box six, praise God for your favorite animal.** Distribute animal crackers.

Say: **On the last day of Creation, God rested. Let's put a marshmallow pillow in box seven to remind us of that day.**  Distribute marshmallows. **After God created everything, he said it was very good. Let's see how good our snack is! As you eat, call out words that describe God's wonderful creation.** Have kids eat.

CLEAN EARTH

Best All Ages For

A skit about how we sometimes treat God's earth.

SCRIPTURE

Genesis 1:31

PROPS

- a chair or stool
- a sign to be hung around someone's neck that reads "EARTH"
- an empty, disposable coffee cup
- a piece of chewing gum
- a bag with crumpled up paper and candy wrappers in it
- a garbage bag
- a sponge

CAST

- EARTH, dressed in blue and white, with a sign that reads "EARTH" around his or her neck
- Person One, chewing a piece of gum and holding a coffee cup
- Person Two, carrying a bag with crumpled up paper and candy wrappers
- Girl, carrying a garbage bag and a sponge

BEHIND THE SCENES

This is a simple skit, with an easy setup and no dialogue. The actor playing "EARTH" will use very animated facial expressions.

 **Action!**

➜ *The skit begins with EARTH seated center stage. He looks down at the sign that reads "EARTH" around his neck, and smiles.*

Person One walks on stage carrying a disposable coffee cup. He takes one last drink of his coffee and then tosses the cup into EARTH's lap.

Person One then blows a big bubble with his bubble gum, letting it pop on his face. He takes the gum out and sticks it onto EARTH's sleeve. EARTH's smile fades a little—it's as though EARTH is trying to make the best of it but is a bit embarrassed now.

Person Two enters with a small plastic bag slung over her shoulder. She walks over to EARTH and pulls out crumpled up papers and candy wrappers, dropping them on EARTH's lap. EARTH doesn't react (except to close eyes). Person Two does this a couple times, making sure EARTH is covered. Then she turns and exits.

EARTH sits—dirty, messy, and looking as sad as he possibly can.

After a long pause, a little girl enters. She's carrying a garbage bag and a sponge. As she interacts with EARTH, she is gentle and careful, treating EARTH very tenderly. She starts by taking the garbage off and putting it in her plastic garbage bag. One piece at a time, she throws the garbage away—makes a face when she reaches the gum, but takes it off just the same.

Next, she goes around to EARTH's back and pretends to clean it, using the sponge. She pulls more garbage off and puts it in the garbage bag. Finally, she takes off the sign marked "EARTH" and writes the words "Take care of the" above the word "EARTH" and re-hangs it around EARTH's neck.

The girl exits, and as she does, EARTH springs to life, picks up the sign around his neck and smiles—hams up being grateful to the exiting girl.

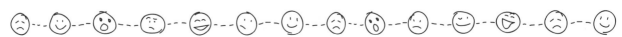

GOD HAS GIVEN US THIS WORLD

BEST
All Ages **FOR**

Kids learn about God's gift of creation through this descriptive song set to the tune of "Twinkle, Twinkle, Little Star."

SCRIPTURE

Genesis 1

Sing It!

Every boy and every girl
(Point to other kids)

God has given us this world
(Hands folded across chest)

Oceans deep and great big sky
(Hands down as if putting them in water; then hands stretched high and wide)

Forests green and mountains high
(Arms held upright like trees; then touch hands to form a "mountain" shape)

Every boy and every girl
(Point to other kids)

Let's take care of God's big world.
(Hold hands with neighbor.)

Extra Special **FACTOIDS**

DID YOU KNOW...

The earth's estimated weight is 6,585,600,000,000,000,000,000 tons. Plus, the earth isn't a perfect sphere. The earth's rotation causes it to bulge around the equator.

DID YOU KNOW...

Adam Had to Name Them All... Scientists estimate that there are approximately 8.7 million species on planet Earth. According to the journal PLoS Biology, a whopping 86% of all species on land and 91% of those in the seas have yet to be discovered.

CLEAN-UP COMMITTEE

BEST
All Ages
FOR

Kids help bring beauty to God's creation.

SCRIPTURE

Psalm 24:1

WHAT YOU'LL NEED

- Bible
- work gloves
- eco-friendly trash bags

The Experience

Plan to pick up cans, bottles, and trash in your community. Choose a section of town, a park, or several areas, depending on the size of your group, to target for cleanup. If necessary form separate groups with adult leaders as needed.

Gather kids together for your service day. Begin by reading Psalm 24:1.

SAY: **In the beginning, God gave Adam care over all the earth. On Earth Day, we acknowledge God as Creator and honor him by taking care of what he made.**

Have kids clean up the designated area. Separate trash from recyclables for disposal.

Afterward, help kids reflect on the experience. Ask kids what it was like to pick up other people's gross trash. Close with a prayer, thanking God for his creation and asking him to help us remember to take care of it.

Extra Special FACTOID

DID YOU KNOW...

The earth has 40 time zones. The most unusual is located in western Australia, east of the town of Caiguna. About 200 people are offset from the rest of the region by 45 minutes.

Mother's Day

Mother's Day isn't only an American holiday; celebrations honoring mothers have taken place for centuries, including a holiday in 1600s England when early Christians celebrated a day honoring Jesus' mother, Mary. That special day was later expanded to include all mothers. Today, cultures everywhere celebrate moms and special women who serve as moms. With these Mother's Day ideas, kids will honor their mothers and those special women in their lives as they recognize the blessings they give us.

Devotion
The Best Mom
page 74

Craft
Mom's-a-Gem Wordle
page 75
Mom's Coffee Sleeves
page 76

Game
She Knows Me So Well
page 77

Snack
Soup for Mom
page 78

Skit
My Amazing Mom
page 79

Song
I Love You, Yes I Do
page 81
God Gave Me a Mother
page 82

Outreach
Mom's Helping Hands
page 83

The Best Mom

BEST
Upper Elementary
FOR

Kids learn just how noble their mothers are.

SCRIPTURE

Proverbs 31:13-29

WHAT YOU'LL NEED

• Bibles
• paper
• pens

The Experience

Form small groups of kids, having no more than 17 groups. Split the verses of Proverbs 31:13-29 among the groups as evenly as possible.

SAY: **The Bible has a lot to say about moms. You've each got Bible verses about awesome moms. A lot of this passage talks about what moms did back in Bible times. Maybe moms today don't do all those things anymore—but they do similar things. Your job is to read your verses and see if you can spot anything that reminds you of *your* mom or someone who's like a mom to you. For example, verse 13 says, "She finds wool and flax and busily spins it." Maybe your mom does some sewing, or maybe she takes you to buy clothes.**

Allow time for kids to read and think about their verses. Then distribute paper and pens, and have kids rewrite their verses to better describe today's moms.

ASK: **What did you notice about how moms' roles have changed or stayed the same?**

• What do you most appreciate about what your mom does?

When kids are finished, have them come up to the front of the room and stand in a line in order of their verses. Then go down the line, letting kids read the rewritten verses. Practice a few times. Then plan a time for mothers to come in to see the presentation, or see if you can snag a few minutes onstage during the main service for kids to present their verses to the church.

Tip If you're planning to have kids present in front of the church, encourage them to bring in props that help demonstrate their rewritten verses.

BEST
Elementary
FOR

Mom's-a-Gem Wordle

Moms are more precious than rubies—and this craft will show them just how precious they are.

SCRIPTURE

Proverbs 31:10

WHAT YOU'LL NEED

- computer
- color printer
- Internet access
- paper
- pens or pencils
- inexpensive 8½x11 frames (available at many dollar and craft stores)
- stick-on gems
- Wikki Stix or Bendaroos craft sticks

The Experience

<u>SAY:</u> **Our moms are gems! Proverbs 31:10 says this about a good mom: "She is more precious than rubies." Rubies are very valuable red jewels or gems. Our moms are special and precious to us. Take a few minutes to think of words that describe your mom, a grandmother or aunt, or another woman in your life who takes care of you. To help you get started,** think of words that could finish this sentence: "My mom is..." Write those words.

Hand out paper and pencils. Allow time.

<u>SAY:</u> **Now we're going to add your word list into a computer program that's going to make a super-cool word collage called a Wordle. You'll need at least 12 words to make your Wordle look cool. The more words, the better it'll turn out. Then we'll put it into a picture frame and you'll get to decorate the frame and give it on Mother's Day.**

When kids have their word lists, visit wordle.net and click "Create your own."

Type a child's words into the box called "Paste in a bunch of text." Click "Go." If kids want certain words to appear larger than others, type in those words multiple times. The more you enter a word, the larger it'll appear.

Let kids each choose a font, layout, and color scheme. Then print the Wordles.

Help kids put their unique Wordles into frames, and then let them decorate the picture frames with stick-on gems and Wikki Stix or Bendaroos craft sticks.

Tip If you don't have access to a computer and Internet in your room, do this a week in advance and take kids' lists home to do this. On Mother's Day, hand out the Wordles to the kids, and have them decorate their frames.

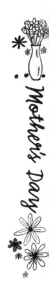

Mother's Day

Mom's Coffee Sleeves

Kids make keepsake coffee cup sleeves moms will treasure.

SCRIPTURE

Proverbs 23:25

WHAT YOU'LL NEED

- Bible
- cardboard coffee cup sleeves (available at grocery stores and coffee shops)
- pens
- different-colored 9x12-inch craft foam sheets
- scissors
- markers
- assorted foam stickers
- ½-inch adhesive Velcro strips

The Experience

Read aloud Proverbs 23:25. <u>SAY:</u> **Raise your hand if your mom works hard.** Pause. **Moms have a lot to do, and one thing that many moms like is coffee—because it keeps them energized. So we're going to make coffee sleeves to help our moms keep up their energy.**

1. Pull open the cardboard coffee sleeves, and use the cardboard as a template for kids to trace onto the craft foam. Help the kids cut out their sleeve shapes.

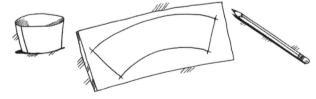

2. Have kids write a message on the coffee sleeves. For example, kids could write "Happy Mother's Day" or "I Love You, Mom" and decorate the foam sleeves with foam stickers.

3. Have kids stick Velcro strips on the ends of the sleeves so the ends overlap approximately ¾-inch and stick together.

Encourage kids to take home their sleeves as a great gift for Mom.

End by praying as a group for all kids' mothers. Pray that God will give mothers the energy they need to do all the things that keep them busy.

She Knows Me So Well

BEST
Elementary
FOR

Kids will discover just how much their moms love them with this game.

SCRIPTURE

Matthew 6:25-32

WHAT YOU'LL NEED

- Bible
- 5 items, each of a very different shape and weight; for example, a pair of balled-up socks, a golf ball, a set of keys, a beach ball, and a Frisbee toy

The Experience

SAY: **On Mother's Day, we celebrate moms. And if anyone deserves a celebration, it's moms. Some days we ask our moms, "When will I eat?" or "What can I do?" or "What should I wear?" Listen to what the Bible says about what we need.** Read Matthew 6:25-32. **We're important to God—and we're important to our moms, too. Like God, our moms love us and know exactly what we need exactly when we need it. In fact, they might even know what we need before we ask.**

Let's take a minute and think of all the things that moms give us or do for us when we need it. Allow one minute for kids to call out ideas.

SAY: **I'm going to give you a chance to see how much moms love us and how they give us everything we need.**

Form a circle and let each child say his or her name so others know it. Toss one of the items around the circle in a pattern, saying the name of the person you're about to toss the item to. Let kids get comfortable with the pattern—it should feel easy. After a few times around, add one more item. Toss the second item right after the first in a rhythm. After a few tries, add in another item… then another…and another! If a child drops the item, he or she picks it up quickly and continues the pattern. After a few rounds, gather the items.

ASK: **What was easy or difficult about this game?**

- **How is this game like or unlike what moms do for us?**

- **How can we thank our moms for all they do to take care of us?**

SAY: **One thing that moms are never too busy for…is a hug! So be sure to give yours a good, long, heartfelt hug today.**

Soup for Mom

BEST
For All Ages

Kids will make this meal for later to save their moms the trouble of cooking on Mother's Day.

ALLERGY ALERT
See p. 7

SCRIPTURE

Exodus 20:12

WHAT YOU'LL NEED

- Bible
- mailing labels
- 1 lb. dried lentils
- 1 lb. split green peas
- 1 lb. pearl barley
- 1 lb. brown rice
- 1 lb. alphabet macaroni
- 2 cups instant onion flakes
- large bowl
- stirring spoon
- measuring cups
- resealable sandwich bags
- index cards
- markers
- tape

The Experience

Preprint the following instructions on mailing labels: "Add 6 cups of water, and simmer for 1½ hours. Add fresh ingredients if desired, such as celery, shredded cabbage, tomatoes, or leftover meat."

SAY: **Today we're celebrating Mother's Day.**

Read aloud Exodus 20:12.

ASK: **What can you do to honor your mother?**

SAY: **One way we can honor our moms is to help with dinner. We're going to make something that'll honor your moms by helping them.**

Have kids help you pour all of the food ingredients into a large bowl and stir them. Then have each child scoop 1½ cups of the mixture into a sandwich bag.

Give each child a preprinted label to stick to his or her bag.

Then have kids write or draw coupons on index cards describing how they'll help with the meal, such as stirring the pot, setting the table, or doing the dishes. Have kids attach their coupons on the bags of soup mix and give them to their moms as Mother's Day gifts.

SAY: **Giving back to our moms is one way we honor our parents, just like God tells us to do. Let this Mother's Day be a reminder for you to help and honor your mom—all year-round.**

Extra Special FACTOID

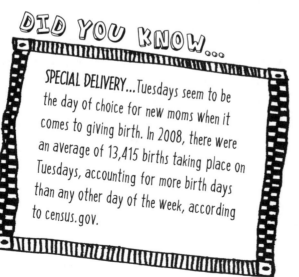

DID YOU KNOW...

SPECIAL DELIVERY...Tuesdays seem to be the day of choice for new moms when it comes to giving birth. In 2008, there were an average of 13,415 births taking place on Tuesdays, accounting for more birth days than any other day of the week, according to census.gov.

BEST
All Ages
FOR

My Amazing Mom

Mother's Day

Kids work together to discover how amazing moms are.

PROPS

• no props needed

CAST

• Leader

BEHIND THE SCENES

This interactive skit has kids in groups of four, moving and talking about their moms' amazing characteristics. This skit works best if the audience has space to move about the room without chairs or tables obstructing them.

Action!

➡ *The Leader comes out to center stage and gathers the audience into groups of four.*

LEADER

My mom is amazing. Now it's true that moms do a lot for us. In fact, without moms or women who serve as moms, none of us would even be here. Our clothes wouldn't match, we'd miss soccer practice, and we'd eat potato chips for every meal. But more than just doing stuff, I know *my* amazing mom means a whole lot more. First, she's honest. I know I can count on my mom being honest and true. In your groups, with all of your hands, come up with a math problem you know is true.

➡ *Show the kids the example, "1 + 1 = 2" by using fingers for both the numbers and the plus and equals signs.*

LEADER

And my amazing mom is honorable! That means she does what's right, and she knows the difference between what's right and what's wrong. In your groups, some show me how to stand up tall the right way, and some show me an opposite—or wrong—way to stand up tall.

➡ *Encourage kids to get really wacky with their stances. After a few seconds, have the kids switch who's doing normal and wacky stances.*

LEADER

And my amazing mom is just! "Just" means she's fair. Face someone in your group and show that person what your face looks like when things are unfair.

➡ *Allow about 10 seconds for kids to do this.*

LEADER

My mom is also very, very lovely. I think she's so pretty! Right now, walk around the room as if you were the prettiest person in here.

➡ *Allow about 20 seconds for kids to do this. Then continue.*

LEADER

She also is kind. That means she talks nice about people and tells everyone when I do something good. In your groups, turn to someone and tell about a time your mom bragged on you.

➡ *Allow about two minutes for kids to talk. Then continue.*

LEADER

And last, my mom's heart is SO big and SO full of virtue and praise. Virtue means "goodness," and boy, is my mom full of goodness. She loves me and lets me know every day. In your groups, on the ground, use your bodies to create the biggest heart shape you can.

➡ *Allow about one minute for kids to do this. Then conclude the skit with the last line.*

LEADER

So when I think about my mom, I'm going to think about her as true, honorable, just, lovely, kind, and good.

 BEST All Ages FOR

I Love You, Yes I Do

Kids can thank their moms with these simple lyrics, set to the tune of "Frère Jacques."

SCRIPTURE

Exodus 20:12

Sing It!

Special mommy, special mommy
(Hold out right hand and then left hand),

I love you, yes I do!
(Place right hand on heart; then place left hand on heart.)

On this day you'll know it
(Point a finger to the side of their heads)

'Cause I'll really show it
(Hold their arms wide out to the sides)—

I love you, yes I do!
(Place right hand on heart; then place left hand on heart.)

Extra Special
FACTOIDS

Mother's Day

DID YOU KNOW...

Anna Jarvis loved her mother. Anna watched her mom accomplish amazing things—founding clubs to help mothers in five U.S. cities, working tirelessly to improve work conditions at factories for women, and helping both the North and South by clothing and bandaging Union and Confederate soldiers. On May 12, 1907, two years after her mother's death, Anna held a memorial to her mother and started a campaign to make "Mother's Day" a nationally recognized holiday. She finally succeeded seven years later in 1914.

DID YOU KNOW...

After successfully creating the holiday, Anna found that the day she envisioned, one of reflection and quiet prayers of thanks for all mothers did, was becoming something completely different. She filed a lawsuit to stop the over-commercialization of Mother's Day...which she lost.

Song

God Gave Me a Mother

BEST
Preschool
FOR

Kids can thank God for their moms with these simple lyrics, set to the tune of "On Top of Old Smokey."

Exodus 20:12

Sing It!

For when I am lonely
   (Kids cup hands around eyes, as if looking for someone),

When I hurt my knee
   (Kids hold one knee),

God gave me a mother
   (Kids put hands over heart)

To take care of me.
   (Kids hold up both hands.)

She gives me some kisses
   (Kids "throw" kisses with both hands),

She gives me some love.
   (Kids wrap their arms around themselves.)

God gave me a mother
   (Kids put hands over heart)

From heaven above.
   (Kids hold up both hands.)

Extra Special FACTOID

DID YOU KNOW...

MAMAS IN MEXICO

Mother's Day is a "grande" hit in Mexico. On May 10, churches join the celebration with a special service—an orchestra plays "Las Mañanitas" and church members feast on tamales and atole—a drink that typically includes masa (corn hominy flour), water, piloncillo (unrefined whole cane sugar), cinnamon, vanilla, and sometimes chocolate.

Mom's Helping Hands

Encourage the moms of your community by lightening their load.

SCRIPTURE

1 Thessalonians 5:11

WHAT YOU'LL NEED

- Bible
- plain paper or card stock
- pencils
- black markers
- cookie cutters in various shapes and sizes
- construction paper
- stickers
- hole punches
- yarn
- 4-packs of crayons

The Experience

Read aloud 1 Thessalonians 5:11. <u>SAY:</u> **Most moms have their hands full, literally, with kids, so we're going to give the moms in our community a helping hand and encourage them this Mother's Day.** Have kids make coloring books to help moms keep their kids occupied while waiting for appointments.

1. Have kids trace cookie cutter shapes onto paper with a pencil and then retrace the line with a thick, black marker. Have each child make several pages.

2. For the cover of the coloring book, trace kids' hands in the center of construction paper.

3. Let kids decorate the covers with stickers and a title, such as "Mom's Helping Hand."

4. Add a note from your church on the back cover, with "Made by" and your church name.

5. Have kids punch a hole in one corner of each coloring page and then tie the pages together with a piece of yarn.

6. Include a 4-pack of crayons. (You can purchase these online, or you can divide up a larger box into homemade 4-packs. Just wrap a rubber band around them and attach them to the cover with tape.)

7. Distribute the coloring books to local doctors' offices for their waiting rooms.

Mother's Day

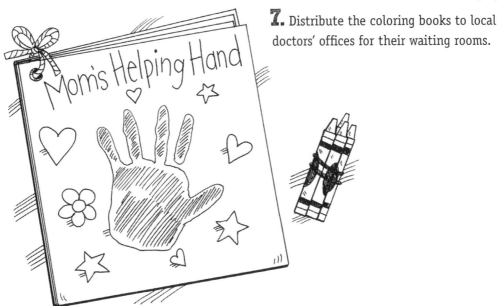

Memorial Day

Remembrance is an important theme in the Bible. The Israelites set up stones of remembrance after crossing the Jordan River. At the Last Supper, Jesus asked his disciples to continue to eat the bread and drink from the cup to remember his sacrifice. Memorial Day is a time set aside for remembering, too. The activities in this section help kids reflect on and honor those who've died to protect them— including Jesus.

Stones of Remembrance

Kids will set up a stone memorial as a way to thank Jesus and others for their sacrifices.

SCRIPTURE

Joshua 4:1-8; John 15:13

WHAT YOU'LL NEED

- Bible
- large rock
- tarp
- fine-tip permanent markers
- stones

The Experience

Before kids arrive, set up a tarp in the corner of the room and write "People Who've Died for Us" on the large rock. Set the rock out of sight.

SAY: **On Memorial Day, we remember people who've served each of us by protecting our country. And we remember the sacrifices of people who died protecting our country.**

Think silently about someone who made a sacrifice for you. Maybe it's something small, like letting you have the last brownie. Or maybe it's something bigger, like a friend who gave you his favorite toy.

Tip If stones are too hard to find, build a rock wall instead by cutting small stone shapes out of construction paper and having kids tape them to the wall. Set the large stone in front of the wall.

As kids think, distribute a stone and marker to each child. SAY: **In the Bible, people sometimes used a pile of stones to remember something special. In Joshua 4, God helped the Israelites get across the Jordan River. To remember what God did for them, the Israelites made a pile of 12 stones by the river. Let's remember the sacrifices you thought of just now the same way. Write or draw about the sacrifice someone made for you on your stone. When you're done, you can come up and set the stone on the tarp.**

After kids have all set their stones on the tarp, read John 15:13. Bring out the large rock and set it in front of the pile of stones.

SAY: **There's one sacrifice that Jesus said was the greatest of all—giving up your life for someone else. This big rock helps us remember that great sacrifice that many men and women have made to keep our country safe. And it helps us remember that Jesus also gave his life for us.**

ASK: **What are some things you can do to remember what soldiers have done for you?**

• **What are some things you can do to remember what Jesus has done for you?**

SAY: **One thing you can do is keep adding to the rock pile. Anytime someone makes a sacrifice for you or God does something really amazing in your life, you can write it on a stone and add it to our pile here.** Place blank stones and permanent markers by the pile so kids can add to it anytime.

Memory Slap Bracelets

Kids make bracelets to wear as a reminder of how God has helped their country.

SCRIPTURE

Psalm 136:24

WHAT YOU'LL NEED

- Bible
- slap bracelets (available at online discount retailers)
- felt
- assorted foam stickers
- a hot glue gun

The Experience

<u>SAY:</u> **Memorial Day is a day of remembering the men and women who died while serving in the United States Armed Forces. We can remember that even though those people gave their lives, their sacrifice has helped keep our country safe. God helps keep our country safe, too.** Read Psalm 136:24.

<u>ASK:</u> **Tell about a person you know who served in the military.** (If kids don't know anyone, share a story about someone you know.)

- **What kinds of sacrifices did that person have to make to serve our country?**

<u>SAY:</u> **Memorial Day is also a time when people remember loved ones who've died, even if they didn't serve in the military.**

<u>ASK:</u> **Tell about someone in your family who has died.**

- **What's your favorite memory about that person?**

- **Why do you think it's important to remember special things about people who've died?**

<u>SAY:</u> **Losing people we love makes us very sad, but we can keep their memories alive. We can do that by making a reminder slap bracelet in honor of that person.**

Hand out slap bracelets and markers. Have kids write the name of a person they shared about and "You are in my heart!" on one side of the bracelet.

Have kids then cut a 9¼x4-inch piece of felt. Help kids fold the felt over the flat slap bracelet and then hot glue it along the outside edges to form a pocket for the slap bracelet. They can then add felt shapes and foam stickers to the outside of the felt.

Encourage kids to keep and wear their bracelets in memory of the special people in their lives who've died. Tell kids that when they see their bracelets, they can remember to thank God for their lost loved ones.

Memorial Day

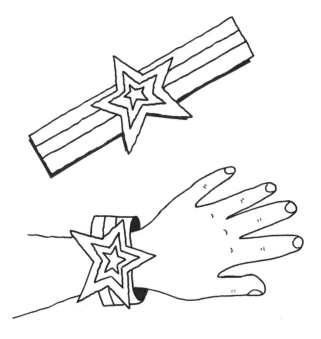

Game

Movement Memory

BEST
Elementary
FOR

Kids are challenged to use their brains in this engaging game.

SCRIPTURE

Deuteronomy 4:9

WHAT YOU'LL NEED

• Bible

Extra Special FACTOID

DID YOU KNOW...

On the Thursday before Memorial Day, soldiers from the 3rd U.S. Infantry (The Old Guard) place small American flags at each of the more than 260,000 gravestones at Arlington National Cemetery. They patrol the cemetery 24 hours a day during the weekend to ensure that each flag remains standing.

The Experience

Stand in a large circle of 10 or more. SAY: **Be careful! Watch closely so you don't forget the things your eyes have seen. Don't let them slip from your heart—as long as you live!**

Say your full name, first and last, while doing some kind of unique movement. For example, you could say your name while lifting your right leg and hitting your knee with your hand for every syllable.

SAY: **Now, let's teach these to our children, and to their children after them.** Have the person to your right repeat your name and action, then say his or her full name and add one unique action. Continue around the circle, having kids each repeat everyone's name and action before them, then adding their name and action.

After making it around the circle, ASK:

• **What was easy or hard about remembering everyone's name and action?**

• **What kinds of things do you think it's important to remember about loved ones?**

Read aloud Deuteronomy 4:9. SAY: **This Scripture is Moses talking to the people of Israel, asking them to follow the Ten Commandments that God just gave him. He was urging the people to never forget what they've seen, and to teach their kids and their kids' kids all about God. It was very important for them to remember what Moses told them. In the same spirit, Memorial Day is a time for us to remember those who've fought and died for our country and our freedoms. We remember why people are willing to die for other people's freedoms.**

Ask kids to tell about any friends or family members they have serving in the armed forces or who've died while serving. Then pray, thanking God for the men and women who've given their lives for our freedom.

Sparkler Pretzels

BEST
All Ages
FOR

Kids celebrate Memorial Day with festive pretzel sparklers.

SCRIPTURE

Psalm 35:27

WHAT YOU'LL NEED

- Bible
- large pretzel rods
- whipped topping or white frosting
- red and blue decorative sugar
- paper plates

The Experience

Give kids each a pretzel rod and help them cover the pretzel with frosting or whipped topping. <u>SAY:</u> **This week, we're celebrating Memorial Day. Memorial Day is a day we remember people who've died, especially those who died serving in the military.**

<u>ASK:</u> **Tell about someone you know who's served in the military.**

• **What are good things military heroes have done for us?**

Read Psalm 35:27. <u>SAY:</u> **We want to celebrate those who've defended our country. Sometimes people use sparklers to celebrate Memorial Day. Let's make pretzel sparklers to remind us of people who sacrifice so much to keep our country safe.** Help the kids sprinkle their pretzels with the red and blue sugars.

<u>SAY:</u> **I'm going to pray for our snack. When I pause, you can say the name of anyone you know who's served our country so we can thank God for that person and the sacrifice he or she made to protect and serve us.**

<u>PRAY:</u> **Dear God, we thank you for keeping our country safe. And we thank you for the people who've served in the military**

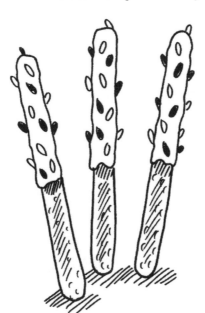

to defend our country, some even giving the ultimate sacrifice with their lives. We thank you for... (pause to let kids fill in names). **And we thank you that you gave your life for us, too. In Jesus' name, amen.**

Memorial Day

Remembered

 BEST All Ages FOR

In this skit, a boy remembers fallen heroes.

SCRIPTURE

Deuteronomy 4:9

PROPS

- a room divider (can be a sheet hung between two poles)
- a bouquet of flowers

CAST

- Soldier 1
- Soldier 2
- Boy

BEHIND THE SCENES

The stage can be divided by either a free-standing room divider or a sheet hung between two poles. Visually, it should look as though the boy is going to a memorial wall of some kind, and the soldiers are behind it—but the audience can see both the boy and the soldiers. The soldiers can be dressed in military uniforms, but this isn't necessary.

 **Action!**

➡ *SOLDIER ONE moves to one side of the divider. SOLDIER TWO enters behind SOLDIER ONE and they salute each other.*

SOLDIER ONE

You made it back, Private. Happy to see you're still in one piece.

SOLDIER TWO

Quite a battle out there, Sir. Enemy attacked in the dead of night. We weren't expecting it.

SOLDIER ONE

You were trained for this. Good work out there, Soldier.

SOLDIER TWO

Thank you, Sir. *(He sighs.)*

SOLDIER ONE

Something on your mind?

SOLDIER TWO

Sometimes I just wonder what we're doing this for, Sir.

SOLDIER ONE

We're fighting the enemy, preserving the greater good.

SOLDIER TWO

But for what, Sir? No one seems to remember that we're here. They go on with their lives back home and we're over here—fighting this war.

SOLDIER ONE

Well, you're right about that, Private—but we don't focus on that. We do our best.

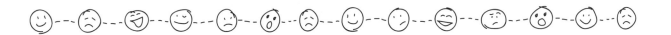

SOLDIER TWO

Our best. *(He sighs.)* **Yes, Sir.**

➡ *Just then, a BOY enters. He is carrying a bouquet of flowers. He kneels down facing the divider as if he's visiting a memorial wall. He situates the flowers on the floor and runs his hand along the divider.*

BOY

Private Harold Taylor.

SOLDIER TWO

Did you hear that, Sir?

SOLDIER ONE

What's that, Private?

SOLDIER TWO

Someone just said my name, Sir.

BOY

Private Taylor, my daddy says you're a hero.

SOLDIER TWO

Me? A hero?

BOY

He says you were my great-grandpa, and you fought in a terrible war. He said you

saved lots of people. They gave you a shiny Purple Heart. It's a medal, and it means you did a really good job.

SOLDIER TWO

A Purple Heart? Me?

BOY

Daddy told me it's Memorial Day, and he brought us to visit you—he makes sure we always remember what you did for us and for our country. Because if it weren't for people like you, we wouldn't be able to do things like worship God in church on Sunday.

➡ *SOLDIER TWO smiles warmly.*

BOY

So, these flowers are for you...to say "thanks." And to tell you that even though I never got to meet you, I'll never forget you. I'm going to tell my own kids all about you someday. *(Pause, and then whispering)* **You're my hero, Grandpa.**

➡ *SOLDIER TWO turns back to SOLDIER ONE.*

SOLDIER ONE

Sometimes, soldier, they do remember.

Memorial Day

Song♪

We Remember

BEST *Preschool* FOR

Kids remember and thank those who gave their lives for freedom with a song set to the tune of "Oh My Darlin', Clementine."

SCRIPTURE

Deuteronomy 4:9

Sing It!

We remember, we remember
(Kids point to their heads, as if thinking)

We remember on this day
(Kids hold up one pointer finger)

That you fought for
(On "fought for," kids hit fist into palm twice)

All our freedom
(Kids hold hands out to sides, palms up)

We remember on this day.
(Kids point to their heads, as if thinking.)

All the soldiers, all the soldiers
(Kids march in place)

We remember on this day
(Kids hold up one pointer finger)

That you died for
(On "died for," kids hit fist into palm twice)

All our freedom
(Kids hold hands out to sides, palms up)

We remember on this day.
(Kids point to their heads, as if thinking.)

Extra Special FACTOIDS

DID YOU KNOW...

Red poppies are recognized as the Memorial Day flower, inspired by a World War I era John McCrae poem, "In Flanders Fields."

DID YOU KNOW...

The very first Memorial Day was celebrated on May 30, 1868. General James Garfield made a speech at Arlington National Cemetery, after which 5,000 participants placed flowers in memoriam of those who'd died on the graves of more than 20,000 Union and Confederate soldiers buried there.

We Will Not Forget

BEST
All Ages
FOR

Kids make a memorial flag to honor those who've lost their lives for our country.

SCRIPTURE

Luke 22:19

WHAT YOU'LL NEED

- red, white, and blue decorative objects, such as buttons, ribbon, fabric scraps, streamers, craft foam shapes, and more
- large white bedsheet
- black, red, and blue fabric markers
- craft glue

The Experience

Several weeks before Memorial Day, contact your local Veterans of Foreign Wars or American Legion for a list of local service members killed in the line of duty. Explain that your group would like to honor their memory for Memorial Day by creating a mural to hang in the organization's building or be on public display for the holiday. Use a black fabric marker to draw an outline of the U.S. flag on the bedsheet.

SAY: **Memorial Day is about remembering the people who've died for us and for our country. The first person who ever died just for you was Jesus. Just before he died, Jesus served his disciples a final meal and told them to continue the practice in his** memory with a special meal. He told them, **"Do this to remember me" (Luke 22:19). Let's remember the people who've died for our country with a special banner.**

1. Have kids decorate the sheet with the red, white, and blue objects to make the shape of the U.S. flag.

2. Have kids fill in the red and blue parts of the flag by using the fabric markers to write the names from the list of those who died in the line of duty.

3. Have one child write the words "We Will Not Forget" above or below the flag with a fabric marker.

4. Have all kids sign their names by those words to show their thanks for the sacrifice.

5. Set up a time you can present the mural to the agency that provided the names, or put the mural on display in your church and invite the members of the agency to come view it at your church's Memorial Day service.

Memorial Day

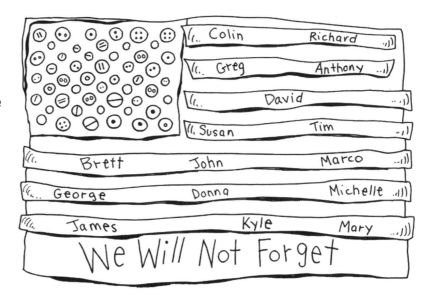

YOUR A SPECIAL DAD
HAPPY FATHER'S DAY
#1 DAD

Throughout the Bible, God calls himself our Father. That means every one of us has a father who loves and cares for us and who wants to be a big part of our lives. And God gave us a really special gift, too: Dads or other special men in our lives who care about us and make a difference in our lives. With these Father's Day activities, kids will appreciate their earthly fathers and special men who serve like fathers, and they'll learn that we all share the most gentle, wonderful Father we could ever imagine!

MR. FIX-IT

BEST
All Ages
FOR

Kids learn that we all have a compassionate Father to appreciate.

SCRIPTURE

Psalm 103:13

WHAT YOU'LL NEED

- Bible
- hammer
- nails
- duct tape
- scissors
- poster board
- permanent markers

The Experience

SAY: **Today is Father's Day—so let's talk about dads. Lots of dads make things and fix stuff—broken toilets, wobbly chairs, leaky faucets.** Hold up a hammer and nails and ASK:

• **What things could we make or fix with these?**

Hold up a roll of duct tape and ASK:

• **What could we make or fix with this?**

• **Why do you think some fix-it jobs need duct tape and some need a hammer and nails?**

• **Why do dads need to be tough sometimes and other times be tender and caring?**

SAY: **Dads might use duct tape, glue, nails, or even bandages to fix things. And the Bible tells us we *all* have a Father who's great at fixing things—even the really big things—and who wants to help us. That's because God is a father to us.** Read aloud Psalm 103:13.

ASK: **How do you think God is like or unlike a dad?**

• **What kinds of things can God fix in our lives?**

Hold up the hammer and SAY: **It's good to remember God's power and might.** Hold up the duct tape. **But don't forget that God is tender, gentle, and compassionate to us. The duct tape is powerful.** Cut off a piece of duct tape and let a few kids try to pull it apart like they're playing tug of war. **But it's also soft and doesn't break anything.** Let everyone touch the non-sticky side of the tape to feel how soft and smooth it is.

SAY: **Let's use this duct tape to show how much we love God.**

Use duct tape to write "DAD" on the poster board. (If you have a lot of kids, make multiple poster boards.) Have kids write words of thanks to God on the duct tape, as a prayer of praise to their gentle and compassionate heavenly Father.

△ ▽ △ ▽ △ ▽ △ ▽ (Craft) ▽ △ ▽ △ ▽ △ ▽

PEEK-A-BOO DAD

BEST For All Ages

Kids reveal the ways dads stay busy to help them.

SCRIPTURE

Proverbs 10:1

WHAT YOU'LL NEED

- Bible
- 1 copy per child of "Peek-a-Boo Dad Symbols" handout on page 153
- 1 copy per child of symbols on page 152
- colored card stock
- scissors or X-ACTO blade and cutting mat
- glue sticks
- markers or crayons

The Experience

Before kids arrive, copy the handout on page 152 onto card stock, and cut out the shapes. Copy the handout on page 153 onto card stock, and use scissors or an X-ACTO blade to cut along three sides of each square. Keep one side attached so there are nine flaps.

<u>SAY:</u> **Father's Day is a time to celebrate the dads in our lives— our own dads, our grandfathers and uncles, and other men in our lives who make a difference. Let's hear what the Bible has to say about how God wants us to treat those men.** Read Proverbs 10:1.

<u>ASK:</u> **Based on this verse, what do you think you can do to bring joy to your dad?**

<u>SAY:</u> **Fathers in the Bible did all kinds of things with their sons and daughters. They traveled together. They ate together. They herded sheep together. They fished together. They sat around the fire together. They built things together. Jesus' father Joseph taught him all about carpentry.**

<u>ASK:</u> **What kinds of things do you do with your dad?**

<u>SAY:</u> **Let's show our dads or the special men in our lives how great they are at loving us and helping us in all kinds of ways.** Spread the cutouts of the symbols on the workspace, and distribute the paper with flaps cut out. **Take a look at all these pictures and choose the ones that remind you of your dad or another special guy. Then glue each one to the outside of a flap. On the inside of the flap, draw or write a message that relates to that picture.**

When kids are done, <u>SAY:</u> **Give your dad this craft and show him each flap as you thank him for all he does for you.**

FATHER'S DAY

△ ▽ △ ▽ △ ▽ △ ▽ (Craft) ▽ △ ▽ △ ▽ △ ▽ △

Game

FEATS OF STRENGTH

BEST *All Ages* FOR

Kids experience a series of interactive challenges that test their strength—and get them talking about how strong their dads really are.

WHAT YOU'LL NEED

• no supplies needed

The Experience

Have kids form pairs. SAY: **We're going to discover how strong you are by trying a series of challenges. Your first challenge? One-Legged Elbow Wrestling!** Have partners interlock their right elbows and hold one foot off the ground at the same time. **When you say "go," kids will attempt to push their partners off balance. The challenge ends when the first person in each pair has to put his or her foot down to keep from falling. Allow time.**

Have kids switch partners. SAY:

Next? Flat-Bottomed Back Wrestling! Have kids sit on the floor, back-to-back and elbows interlocked, with their knees raised close to the chest. **On "go," the first person to get his or her partner's right shoulder to touch the ground wins. Ready, go!** Allow time.

Have kids switch partners again. SAY: **Last? The Toe-to-Toe Hand Pull!** Have kids sit on the floor facing their partners with toes touching. SAY: **Interlink both your hands with your partner's hands. On "go," try to lift your partner off the ground by pulling back on his or her hands.**

The challenge is over when one person leaves the ground. Ready, go! Allow time.

Once kids complete all three challenges, encourage them to share which events they were strongest in. Applaud everyone's efforts.

ASK: **Tell about a time you felt strong.**

• Other than physical strength, what are ways people are strong?

• Who's the strongest person you know— and what makes that person so strong?

SAY: **Father's Day is a day we recognize all the great things about our dads including their physical, emotional, mental, and spiritual strength. Father's Day is also a day to recognize we have an amazing, strong, and powerful Father in heaven—God, who loves us very much and is stronger than anyone.**

Close in prayer, thanking God for being a strong Father and for giving kids great dads and men in their lives.

OUR FATHER

BEST
All Ages
FOR

Kids eat a snack that helps them understand how special fathers are—including our heavenly Father.

SCRIPTURE

Genesis 17:4;
Matthew 6:9;
Romans 8:15-16

ALLERGY ALERT *See p. 7*

WHAT YOU'LL NEED

- Bible
- Chex Mix snack mix
- Starburst candies
- wafer cookies
- frosting
- plastic knives

The Experience

SAY: **Father's Day is a time to celebrate the dads in our lives and to remember God, too. Did you know there are more than 1,000 verses about fathers in the Bible? We're going to look at three of them and eat a snack that helps us understand each one.**

The first verse is from the Old Testament. God tells Abraham he has big plans for him. Invite a child to read Genesis 17:4. Hand out Chex Mix. **There are many different kinds of ingredients in Chex Mix, and that can remind us of the many children Abraham had. Just think—some of us might be Abraham's great-great-great-great-great-times-a-million-grandchildren!** Let kids eat their Chex Mix.

ASK: **What's something special you can think of about your grandpa or your great-grandpa?**

SAY: **Here's another verse where Jesus teaches us how to pray.** Read Matthew 6:9. **When Jesus taught his followers to pray, he started by calling God "Our Father." And Jesus recognized that God was our Father in heaven.** Distribute Starburst candies. **Starburst candies remind us of the stars in the sky, which help us remember just how big and amazing God is.** Let kids eat their candies.

ASK: **Tell about one way God has shown you how big he is.**

SAY: **Here's the last verse.** Read Romans 8:15-16. **The word** *abba* **is a Greek word that is a special word children could use to talk to their fathers. It's very personal, like our word** *daddy*. Distribute the wafer cookies, frosting, and plastic knives. **Stick two cookies together with frosting to remember just how close you are to God.** Let kids eat their cookies.

ASK: **How is God like your daddy?**

• **Why do you think God wants us to feel so close to him?**

SAY: **This Father's Day, remember to thank your dad or someone who loves you like a dad for the way he shows you God's love. And remember that all of us—even people whose dads aren't with them—have a heavenly Father who loves us very much.**

FATHER'S DAY

Snack

ROLE REVERSAL

 BEST FOR All Ages

A dad and his son switch roles.

Scripture

Galatians 4:6

Props

• no supplies needed

Cast

• Dad
• Son

Behind the Scenes

The stage can be empty, just Dad and Son in the center. Both parts need to be cast with people who are animated, and the dialogue can be spoken rather quickly—but still clearly so the audience can understand.

 **Action!**

➤ *Dad and Son are at center stage.*

DAD

Hey, son.

SON

Hey, Dad.

DAD

You doing well?

SON

Can't complain. You?

DAD

Oh, you know. Good days, bad days. I'm hanging in there.

SON

I have a question.

DAD

Shoot.

SON

What's it like to be a dad?

DAD

Oh! Um...I was thinking you were going to ask me how to throw a football or something...

SON

Because I want to be a good one.

DAD

You do, huh?

SON

Yep.

DAD

Well...maybe the best way is for you to just be one yourself.

SON

Wait. What? I'm going to be a dad?

DAD

No, no, just pretend to be one. Like, switch spots.

SON

Like, you're the kid and I'm the dad?

DAD

Yep!

SON

Sweet! Go to your room!

DAD

Wait, I...

SON

Clean up your mess!

DAD

Hang on just a...

SON

I'm going to complain about my boss!

DAD

Now, wait a second. There's more to being a dad than shouting orders and telling people what to do.

SON

There is?

DAD

Yes. Let's pretend. *(Pretends to be hurt)* Ow! Ow! *(Wincing)* I twisted my ankle.

SON

Walk it off.

DAD

Hey! I'm serious here.

SON

Okay, let me take a look.

DAD

Ow! It hurts. Be careful.

SON

Let me see. Hmm. Dear Lord, I pray for my son's ankle...

DAD

Wait. What are you doing?

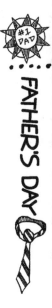

SON

Praying. It's what you do when I'm hurt.

DAD

I do?

SON

Yep.

DAD

(Smiles) Okay, how about this one?
(Switching gears to more animated) Dad! Dad,
can we play a game?

SON

Can't. Football's on.

DAD

Hey, I'm serious here!

SON

Okay, okay. Tell you what. Let's go
outside, just you and me, and spend
some quality time together. How about
that?

DAD

I said that?

SON

Yep. Yesterday.

DAD

Wow. I'm a great dad.

SON

Yeah. You are. So basically, all I have to
do to be a good dad is to...do what you
do.

DAD

Yeah. I guess so. So can we switch back
now?

SON

No. I'm going to take the car for a drive.

➡️ *He turns and quickly starts to exit.*

DAD

Hey! Bad dad! I mean, son! Get back
here!

I'VE GOT A FATHER

BEST *Preschool* FOR ....

A song about God our Father, sung to the tune of "I'm a Little Teapot."

....

SCRIPTURE

1 John 3:1

Sing It!

I've got a Father

(Kids point thumb to chest, indicating "me")

Big and strong

(Kids show muscles)—

He loves me my

(Kids put hands over hearts)

Whole life long.

(On each word, kids point left, center, right.)

When I need a hand

(Kids hold out right hand)

Just hear me shout

(Kids hold hands up to mouth and shout the word "shout"):

My God in heaven can

(Kids point up)

Help me out!

(Kids point thumb to chest, indicating "me.")

Extra Special FACTOIDS

DID YOU KNOW...

Sonora Smart Dodd conceived the idea of Father's Day in Spokane, Washington, while she listened to a Mother's Day sermon in 1909. Dodd (now known as "the mother of Father's Day") wanted a special day to honor her father, William Smart, a widowed Civil War veteran who single-handedly raised his six children on a farm.

DID YOU KNOW...

In most languages, regardless of the pronunciation of the actual word in that language, small children first call their fathers "da-da"—the origin of the English word *dad*.

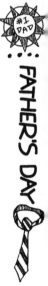
FATHER'S DAY

TREASURE TIES

Show kindness to the dads in your community with these fun tie bookmarks.

SCRIPTURE

Proverbs 3:3

WHAT YOU'LL NEED

- Bible
- card stock
- adhesive Velcro strips
- foam board
- markers
- "Treasure Ties" handout on page 154
- scissors

The Experience

Copy the "Treasure Ties" handout onto various colors of card stock, and cut out the tie shapes. Make arrangements with places of business or a YMCA to hang up encouraging posters.

SAY: **Today's dads can get bogged down by worries and stress over providing for their families and working long hours. They need a little encouragement!** Read Proverbs 3:3. **Let's tie kindness around the necks of the dads in our community with a fun poster board!**

Give kids markers to decorate the tie shapes with fun patterns, and have them write encouraging messages on each tie, such as, "We're glad you're a dad!" or "Dads are great!"

As kids work, stick pieces of Velcro on each piece of foam board, leaving room to stick a tie to each piece. Write, "Dads: Please take a Bookmark Tie!" on the foam board. Have kids attach a piece of Velcro to the upper back of each tie and stick each onto the foam board.

Deliver the boards to various businesses or a local YMCA so dads around your community can take tie bookmarks and feel appreciated.

Extra Special FACTOID

DID YOU KNOW...

The most common gift associated with Father's Day? The necktie. The second most common gift is—wait for it—flowers.

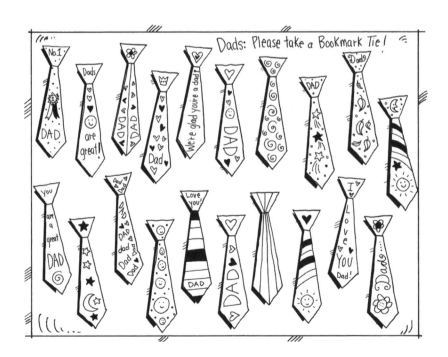

INDEPENDENCE DAY

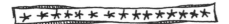

Freedom. This great biblical principle is captured from the Israelites' exodus from Egypt all the way through the letters of the New Testament declaring our freedom in Jesus. Christians experience spiritual freedom knowing Jesus is their Savior, and through him eternal life abounds. Kids will celebrate their freedom—and our freedom in Jesus—with these Independence Day activities.

UNTIED

As kids get untied from a knot, they learn about finding freedom in Jesus.

SCRIPTURE

Romans 8:2

WHAT YOU'LL NEED

• Bible

The Experience

SAY: **On Independence Day we celebrate our freedom! To explore what it means to be free, let's see what it's like "knot" to be free.**

Form a circle. Have kids put their right hand in the center and take hold of the right hand of another person. Then have kids put their left hand in the circle and grab the left hand of another person, but not the same person they're already holding hands with.

While kids are in the knot, have them attempt to scratch their heads, touch their toes, and rub their bellies. Have kids remain in the knot while you discuss the following.

ASK: **Talk about a time you couldn't do what you wanted to do.**

SAY: **Years ago the people who started our country were a lot like you are now in this** circle. **They weren't free. They were ruled by another country across the ocean.**

ASK: **How does our knot show what it's like to not be free?**

Have kids work to unravel the knot without letting go of the hands they're holding. This will be difficult and take time for them to do. After a minute, have kids pause where they are.

ASK: **What are some things you could do to set yourselves free right now?**

SAY: **Many countries in the world celebrate their independence with a big party.** Have the kids shout hooray and let go of one person's hand.

SAY: **Today there's another kind of independence we can celebrate, too. This one comes from the Bible.** Open your Bible and read Romans 8:2.

ASK: **What do you think it means to live free from the power of sin?**

Have kids let go of the other person's hand and then jump around to celebrate their freedom. SAY: **On Independence Day, we can celebrate because our country is free and we're free to live as Christians—free from sin!**

PRAY: **Dear God, thank you for the freedom we celebrate on Independence Day and every day. Thank you that you've set us free from the power of sin. In Jesus' name, amen.**

PARADE WANDS

BEST Elementary FOR

Kids create wands to celebrate how Jesus makes us free.

SCRIPTURE

John 8:36

WHAT YOU'LL NEED

- Bible
- paint sticks
- blue 3-inch foil stars
- red, white, and blue crepe paper
- wired star garland (available at craft stores)
- star stickers
- Avery 5160 mailing labels
- glue dots

The Experience

Before kids arrive, create vertical labels that say "Jesus Set Me Free," using an Avery 5160 label template onto Avery 5160 labels. (See sample below.) Print one per child. Pre-cut 12-inch lengths of red, white, and blue crepe paper and wired star garland.

JESUS SET ME FREE	JESUS SET ME FREE	JESUS SET ME FREE	JESUS SET ME FREE	JESUS SET ME FREE	JESUS SET ME FREE	JESUS SET ME FREE	JESUS SET ME FREE	JESUS SET ME FREE	JESUS SET ME FREE
JESUS SET ME FREE	JESUS SET ME FREE	JESUS SET ME FREE	JESUS SET ME FREE	JESUS SET ME FREE	JESUS SET ME FREE	JESUS SET ME FREE	JESUS SET ME FREE	JESUS SET ME FREE	JESUS SET ME FREE
JESUS SET ME FREE	JESUS SET ME FREE	JESUS SET ME FREE	JESUS SET ME FREE	JESUS SET ME FREE	JESUS SET ME FREE	JESUS SET ME FREE	JESUS SET ME FREE	JESUS SET ME FREE	JESUS SET ME FREE

ASK: Describe what your family will do to celebrate Independence Day.

SAY: To be independent means to be free or to be able to do what you choose to do. On Independence Day, we celebrate our country being free to make our own choices. If you believe in Jesus, you're free, too. Read John 8:36.

ASK: What are differences between the people of our country being free and the way we're free through Jesus?

1. Spread out the craft supplies.

2. Have kids each stick their mailing labels onto a blue foil star.

3. Have kids use a few glue dots to stick the blue foil star to the paint stick, about an inch from the top.

4. Show kids how to twist the garland around red, white, and blue crepe paper and secure it to the top of the paint stick.

5. Let kids add as many star stickers as they'd like to decorate the sticks.

6. After kids make their wands, go on a "Jesus Set Me Free Parade" by marching around the room and waving the wands as you repeat John 8:36 with kids.

INDEPENDENCE DAY

STREAMER CELEBRATION

BEST
All Ages
FOR

....

Kids play a high-energy twist on Tag, using streamers and celebration.

....

SCRIPTURE

Psalm 20:5, Jeremiah 31:13

WHAT YOU'LL NEED

- Bible
- mylar streamers (any color)
- crepe paper streamers (any color)

The Experience

SAY: **On Independence Day, we celebrate our country's freedom—a long-fought battle and a huge victory. You know, the book of Psalms and the book of Jeremiah in the Bible tell us great ways to celebrate victory.** Read aloud Psalm 20:5 and Jeremiah 31:13.

ASK: **What did you hear in those verses that sounds like a celebration we might have today?**

- **What's your favorite way to celebrate?**

SAY: **Let's play a game to celebrate like these verses say. We'll celebrate our country's victory and the joy and freedom we have. And you'll look like a sky full of fireworks in the process!**

Choose three kids to be "It," and tie a 3-foot strip of mylar streamer to the wrist of each It. Have each It roll up the rest of the streamer and hold it in his or her hand. Hand out two 3- to 5-foot pieces of crepe paper streamer to each remaining child. Explain that this game is a bit like Tag, except It has to tag the other kids by throwing and unrolling a mylar streamer. Whenever kids are tagged by a mylar streamer, they have to throw their streamers in the air and celebrate as the Scriptures previously read described. SAY: **If you're tagged, celebrate loudly! Ready? Go!**

Play this wild, firecracker game several times, switching kids' roles so everyone gets a turn to be It.

Extra Special FACTOIDS

DID YOU KNOW...

The first Independence Day celebration in the United States was in 1776—but it was celebrated on July 8th, not the 4th.

DID YOU KNOW...

The names of those who signed the Declaration of Independence were withheld from the public for more than six months to protect the signers. Why, you wonder? If we hadn't actually achieved independence, the treasonable act of the signers would have, by law, resulted in their deaths.

FRUIT FLAGS

Kids will make a fun flag snack as they learn about what the United States flag represents for our country and for our faith.

SCRIPTURE

Ephesians 1:7; John 17:23

ALLERGY ALERT See p. 7

WHAT YOU'LL NEED

- Bible
- graham crackers
- whipped topping or white frosting
- blueberries
- strawberries sliced into long, thin strips
- napkins or paper plates
- plastic knives
- small American flag

The Experience

Distribute a napkin or plate with a graham cracker on it to each child. Hold up the small flag. SAY: **Today we're going to make our own United States flags, but these will be special because when we're all done, we get to eat them.** Help kids spread whipped topping or white frosting on the graham crackers.

SAY: **First, we're going to make the stripes. There are actually 13 stripes, one for each of the 13 original colonies. You might not be able to fit 13 stripes, so just put on as many as you'd like to.** Let kids put the strawberries on the crackers for the stripes. **Those 13 original colonies are a big part of why we have our freedom today.**

Tip If you're in a country outside the U.S., simply choose other kinds of fruit to re-create your flag. Give kids information about the significance of each aspect of the flag as you go.

You know, the red strawberries remind me of something else that was red and brought us freedom. Read Ephesians 1:7.

Next, give kids the blueberries. SAY: **The stars on the flag represent all the states that make up America. Go ahead and put a few blueberry stars in the corner of your flag.** Pause. **Those stars are reminders that one of the goals of our country is unity—that's why we're called the *United* States. Living in unity is just what Jesus wants us to do, too. Right before he died for us, he prayed for us.** Read John 17:23.

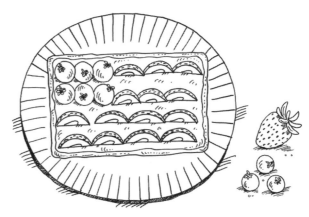

ASK: **Why do you think it's important to be unified?**

- **What are ways you can be unified with your friends?**
- **How do we demonstrate Jesus' love when we're unified with others?**

SAY: **Look at your flag and think about all the freedoms we have—in our country and also because of Jesus. And think about how you can show unity with others. Let's pray about those things.**

PRAY: **Dear God, we're so thankful to have the freedom to worship you however we choose. Help us to show your love by being united with other people. In Jesus' name, amen.**

THE IN-DEEP PEN DANCE

BEST All Ages **FOR**

This skit puts charades in the hands of the audience.

SCRIPTURE

None

PROPS

• none needed

CAST

• 3 actors

BEHIND THE SCENES

This is a different kind of skit, where the audience has to guess collectively what the actors are doing—like large-group charades. The actors need to be animated and full of energy. The script offers suggestions for charades, but feel free to add your own spin!

 Action!

➡ *Three actors stand at center stage. One steps forward, claps four times, and puts a hand to his ear as if to listen for a response. If the audience doesn't respond with four claps in rhythm, the actor claps again, and motions for the audience to repeat. Once the audience has caught on that they're to repeat the rhythm, the actor then changes up the rhythm. For example, two soft claps and then two loud, or two claps and two stomps. The actor can make up a rhythm and end on an involved mixture of stomps and claps that the audience has no way of repeating.*

After the clapping, a second actor steps forward. She holds up her hands to quiet the audience.

ACTOR ONE

Today, we celebrate freedom!

ACTOR TWO

Today, we celebrate liberty!

ACTOR THREE

Today, we celebrate charades!

➡ *The first two actors turn to the third actor with a puzzled look.*

ACTOR THREE

Yes! Jesus died on the cross so that we could be free—and play charades! It's in Matthew. Look it up.

ACTOR ONE

No, it isn't!

ACTOR THREE

Well, it should be. *(Said in a sing-song-y voice and rhythm)* **"Jesus died for all of us that we may have our..."** *(Pause.)* **Argh. I can't tell it any other way than charades.** *(To the other actors)* **Can you help?**

➡ *The other two actors shrug and agree.*

ALL THREE ACTORS

(To audience) **Can *you* help?**

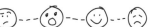

ALL THREE ACTORS

CHARADES!

➡ *The three actors then start by doing three simple charades, one at a time. The first is "PLAYING BASEBALL." The second is "BAKING A CAKE." The third is "WATCHING A MOVIE." Throughout, the actors encourage the audience to shout out collectively what they think it is.*

Once the audience is warmed up to playing the game, ACTOR THREE steps forward.

ACTOR THREE

TRY THIS!

➡ *All three actors gather on the left end of the stage. They're going to act out the word "INDEPENDENCE" in four parts, reading from the audience's left to right.*

The three actors first act out the word "IN." This can be done with two actors joining hands in a circle, while the third actor gets "in" and "out" of the circle. Once the audience guesses "IN," the actors move over.

They then act out the word "DEEP." This can be done by two actors waving their arms like water, and the third actor "wading in." The water actors get higher and higher, until the third actor is underwater, going deeper and deeper. Once the audience guesses "DEEP," the actors move over.

They then act out the word "PEN." This can be done by all three actors pretending to write something. Maybe the pen runs out of ink. Maybe it's a quill pen. Once the audience guesses "PEN," the actors move over.

They then act out the word "DANCE." This can be done by, well, dancing! Once the audience guesses "DANCE," the actors move back to where they acted out "IN."

Then, rather quickly, they act out each of the four words in succession. Running back and forth from one end of the stage to the other, the actors act in such a way that the audience can say "IN…DEEP…PEN…DANCE! IN….DEEP… PEN…DANCE!" faster and faster until the audience is shouting "INDEPENDENCE!"

ALL ACTORS

Yes! *(In the same sing-song-y voice and rhythm)* **Jesus died for all of us so we could have our…***(They indicate to the crowd, prompting them to say the next word all together)* **independence!!**

➡ *Once the crowd gets the final word, all three actors collapse on stage.*

INDEPENDENCE DAY

THE FLAGS ON THE BOAT

BEST
Preschool
FOR ....

A song about Independence Day, sung to the tune of "The Wheels on the Bus." Feel free to add your own verses, or encourage kids to make up their own, based on their experiences with Independence Day. For other countries' days of independence, simply change "fourth" to whatever day you celebrate!

....

SCRIPTURE

John 8:36

Sing It!

The flags on the boat go back and forth
(Kids wave their hands back and forth),

Back and forth, back and forth.
The flags on the boat go back and forth
All on the Fourth!
(Kids clap three times on the beat—once on "All," once on "on," and once on "Fourth!")

The fireworks shoot and pop, pop, bang!
(Kids use hands to imitate fireworks going off.)

Pop, pop, bang! Pop, pop, bang!
The fireworks shoot and pop, pop, bang!
All on the Fourth
(Kids clap three times on the beat—once on "All," once on "on," and once on "Fourth!")

Jesus, he has set me free
(Kids close hands as if in prayer, and then open; repeat each time they sing "Set me free"),

Set me free, set me free.
Jesus, he has set me free
Thanks to you, Lord!
(Kids clap three times on the beat—once on "Thanks," once on "you," and once on "Lord!")

Extra Special FACTOID

DID YOU KNOW...

161 nations around the globe celebrate some kind of independence day, according to aglobalworld.com.

FREE FOR ALL

BEST
All Ages
FOR

Kids discover that the best things in life are free—from the free gift of forgiveness Jesus offers to the free water they give away this Independence Day!

SCRIPTURE

Galatians 5:13

WHAT YOU'LL NEED

- Bible
- bottled water
- mailing labels
- coolers
- wagons
- extra adult volunteers to accompany kids distributing water

The Experience

Find an Independence Day related–event in your area, such as a parade or fireworks show, and plan with kids to give away bottles of water for the event. Determine how much water you need based on the size of the event, and ask church members to sponsor or donate a case of water to offset the cost. Print labels for the water bottles with your church name and contact information, along with a message such as, "The best things in life are free! Enjoy your complimentary water." Or "Freedom isn't free— but this water is! Compliments of [your church]."

Gather coolers and wagons as a way to transport the water if you want to walk through the crowd, or set up a table at a busy intersection for foot traffic or a popular viewing spot. As a courtesy, a couple of weeks prior to the celebration, confirm your plan with the event organizers.

As kids gather and prepare to serve, prepare their hearts by reading Galatians 5:13. SAY: **As Christians, we're called to live free from sin. And we also get to live in a free country. This verse says to use our freedom to serve others in love, so let's do just that!**

Encourage kids to be friendly and outgoing as they hand out the water bottles. Have plenty of extra adult volunteers to accompany kids.

Extra Special
FACTOID

DID YOU KNOW...

Canada remained part of the British Empire until July 1, 1867, when under the British North America Act, Canada East (Quebec), Canada West (Ontario), Nova Scotia, and New Brunswick united to become the Dominion of Canada. Canadians have been celebrating Canada Day every July 1st since.

INDEPENDENCE DAY

Halloween

Halloween is a much-debated holiday among Christians. Many have practical concerns about the safety of trick-or-treating. Others find the celebration of evil spirits a disturbing event for Christians to take part in. And while the holiday has its pagan origins (later redeemed by the Church), it still offers a great opportunity to teach kids important truths. Use these activities to teach kids about discerning good and evil and conquering death with life in Jesus.

Good or Evil?

Good or evil? Kids learn to discern between the two with this optical illusion.

SCRIPTURE

Matthew 7:15; Romans 12:21

WHAT YOU'LL NEED

• a copy of page 155 for each child

The Experience

Give kids each a copy of the "Optical Illusion" handout on page 155. Tell kids they have five seconds to look at the page, and when you call time, they can call out the word they see.

SAY: **There are a lot of things that look harmless or even good. Turn your paper over and hold it up to the light. See if you can read another word.** Help kids look inside the white part of the letters to read the word "evil." SAY: **Sometimes it's hard to tell the difference between good and evil. Sometimes, the devil makes evil look like it's good. But when we hold our decisions up to the light of God's Word, we see the truth about what's good and what's not.**

ASK: **Tell about someone or something you pretended to be either for Halloween or just for fun.**

SAY: **On Halloween, a lot of people dress up in costumes and pretend to be someone or something else. That can be a fun way to celebrate! But Jesus warned us in real life about evil people who pretend to be good. They aren't just having fun.** Read aloud Matthew 7:15. **Sometimes people tell lies about Jesus or do wrong things, but they make it appear to be good. It's kind of like wearing a costume, only it can hurt God.**

ASK: **How is pretending at Halloween different from someone pretending to be good when he or she really isn't?**

• **Without naming names, tell about someone who seemed nice at first, but ended up not being so nice.**

SAY: **On Halloween, it's obvious when people are dressed in a costume. You probably didn't believe there was a real superhero or princess walking down your street! With God's help, telling the difference between good and evil is even easier. It can be just like holding your paper up to the light. And when we can tell good and evil apart, here's what can happen.** Ask a child to read Romans 12:21 aloud to the group.

ASK: **What does it mean to you to conquer evil by doing good?**

• **What are ways God turns bad things into good?**

• **How can you tell which parts of Halloween are good and which are bad?**

SAY: **Halloween is the perfect time to celebrate all the great things God does for us and to celebrate all the goodness in the world. The Bible tells us that God has conquered evil with good. That's something to celebrate!**

Glowing Slime

BEST
Elementary
FOR ....

This gooey, slimy craft helps kids discover how God holds them firmly.

....

SCRIPTURE

1 John 5:18; Matthew 5:16

WHAT YOU'LL NEED

- Bible
- 4 oz. or ½ cup Elmer's white glue or glue gel
- 4% (saturated) Borax powder
- glowing paint or glowing paint powder (available at craft stores)
- water
- spoons
- measuring cups and spoons
- 2 large bowls
- resealable bags
- permanent markers

The Experience

1. Have one child pour the glue into a bowl; then have another add ½ cup warm water.

2. Choose another child to stir the mixture well.

3. Have another child add a couple of squirts of glow-in-the-dark paint or 2 teaspoons of glowing paint powder.

4. In a separate bowl, have kids mix 1 cup water and add 1 teaspoon of Borax powder. Stir well.

5. Slowly stir the glue mixture into the bowl of Borax solution.

6. Give each child some of the slime and have kids knead it under a light source until it feels dry. (Don't worry about excess water remaining in the bowl.) The more kids play with the slime, the firmer and less sticky it'll become.

While kids play, SAY: **Imagine you're the slime. Slime is slippery and hard to hold on to. That's kind of like how the devil tries to hold onto us: We slip right out of his fingers!**

Read aloud 1 John 5:18.

ASK: **How does the way God holds us compare with how you hold your slime?**

- **What does it mean to you that "God's children don't make a practice of sinning"?**

SAY: **When God holds us, he helps us avoid sin and stay out of the devil's grasp. And something else happens to us.** Read aloud Matthew 5:16. Turn out the lights to reveal the glowing slime.

SAY: **On Halloween, it can be easy to focus on evil, scary things. But this Halloween, remember that God is holding your hand, helping you shine with good deeds that show other people how awesome God is.**

Pass out resealable bags and permanent markers, and have kids decorate their bags. Put each child's slime in the bag, and seal it tightly to keep it from evaporating. Clean up as needed with soap and water.

Stomp!

Kids will have some foot-stompin', balloon-poppin' fun.

SCRIPTURE

Romans 8:28

WHAT YOU'LL NEED

- Bible
- dark-colored balloons
- wrapped candies (Jolly Ranchers work well)
- 2-foot lengths of string

The Experience

Gather kids together. Give each child a balloon and a piece of string. Help kids tie one end of the string to the balloon and the other end of the string to their ankle. Although kids might realize something is inside the balloons, don't tell what it is.

SAY: **The object of this game is to pop everyone else's balloon by stomping on them—while keeping your own balloon from being popped. Once your balloon pops, stop where you are and gather the leftover pieces from your popped balloon. Ready? Go!**

Tip PREPARE AHEAD! Before playing, push one wrapped piece of candy inside each balloon, inflate the balloons, and tie them off. Dark-colored balloons work better for this activity because the color prevents kids from seeing the candy. If you don't have dark colors, use thicker balloons.

Play until only one person is left with an unpopped balloon—then have him or her pop it. Once everyone's balloon is popped, have kids "pop" their piece of candy in their mouths.

SAY: **Even though having your balloon popped seemed like a bad thing, what popped out of your balloon was a *good* thing. In life, bad things happen. It might seem like nothing good could *ever* come out of something bad. But here's good news: God can take what's bad and turn it around for good!**

Have kids find a partner to discuss the following questions.

ASK: **What were you thinking when your balloon popped and you discovered a treat inside?**

- **Tell about a time something bad happened in your life.**
- **What good, if any, do you think came out of that bad thing?**

Read aloud Romans 8:28. SAY: **Halloween, October 31st, might seem to some as a "bad day." But like our game, something good can come out of something bad. Halloween is a great time to give, to meet and get to know your neighbors, and to tell people about Jesus. Jesus dying on the cross might've seemed like a bad thing—but *really* it was the most amazing thing ever. God took something bad and turned it into good, and he can do the same in our lives!**

Warning! To avoid choking hazards, be sure to pick up pieces of any broken balloons promptly. Balloons may contain latex.

Pumpkin Pancake Party

BEST
Elementary
FOR

Kids will learn how new life springs from death.

SCRIPTURE

Romans 6:11

ALLERGY
ALERT
See
p. 7

WHAT YOU'LL NEED

- Bible
- instant pancake mix
- eggs
- milk
- canned pumpkin
- cooking spray
- measuring cups and spoons
- electric frying pan or griddle
- spatula
- plates
- forks
- syrup

The Experience

Have kids wash their hands. <u>SAY:</u> **One reason Halloween can be so scary is that it focuses a lot on death. People often dress up as things that symbolize death, like ghosts or goblins. Some people decorate their yards like graveyards. But as Christians, we don't need to fear death. This Halloween, let's see what death means for Christians.**

Preheat the electric frying pan. Invite kids to help you prepare the pancakes by measuring and mixing the ingredients, following the directions on the instant pancake mix. Add ½ cup of canned pumpkin for every cup of instant pancake mix. As you add the pumpkin, <u>SAY:</u> **This canned pumpkin comes from a real, live pumpkin that grew in the ground. The pumpkin died to become our snack. But we're taking a dead pumpkin and turning it into something wonderful—and yummy!**

Spray the griddle or pan with cooking spray if needed. Pour the batter onto the pan. Flip the pancakes when bubbles form. Serve your pancakes with syrup. As kids eat, read Romans 6:11.

<u>ASK:</u> **How does this verse make you think about death?**

• What do you think it means to be dead to the power of sin?

<u>SAY:</u> **Our pumpkin died, but it became something wonderful. That's like what Jesus does in our lives. Through Jesus, we're dead to the power of sin. And we're transformed into life in Jesus! You can honor the death of sin this Halloween by living for Jesus.**

Pumpkin

God's With Matty, Too

BEST For All Ages

Matty's dad reminds him what to do when there's scary stuff around.

SCRIPTURE

Isaiah 41:13

PROPS

- a chair

CAST

- Dad
- Matty
- Mom
- Noisemaker—someone who cues the audience to make noises

BEHIND THE SCENES

This has a basic setup of one chair at center stage—and two actors who don't have any problem being big hams. For the character of Matty, the bigger the reactions, the better! The Noisemaker should stand off to the side of the stage, "unseen" by the actors on the stage but still in view of the audience.

Action!

➡ *Matty is sitting in a chair. His knees are pulled up to his chest and his arms are wrapped around his legs. He is jumpy and scared, but we don't know why. He's looking around, seemingly terrified at the smallest things. Dad enters.*

NOISEMAKER

(Loudly whispers to the audience) **Everyone, on the count of three, stomp your feet on the ground once. One, two, *three!***

➡ *As the audience stomps its feet, Matty jumps up, reacting to the sound. He's terrified, and runs behind the chair to hide. Matty's dad enters, looking around for Matty.*

DAD

Matty? You in here? *(He looks around, but can't find him.)* **Matty? It's bedtime.**

NOISEMAKER

He-he-he! *(Then loudly whispers to the audience)* **On the count of three, everyone say "BUMP!" One, two, *three!***

➡ *At the audience's "bump," Matty comes out from behind the chair, screaming.*

DAD

Whoa, whoa! What's wrong? That was just Buster. He keeps running into the wall.

MATTY

No, that wasn't Buster. That was a monster. A big, huge, green, slimy monster with fangs coming out of its mouth and...

DAD

Whoa, Matty, slow down. There are no monsters.

Halloween

MATTY

I've seen them! Every time you turn out the lights, they're there!

NOISEMAKER

(Loudly whispers to the audience) **On the count of three, everyone say "CRASH" and clap your hands together once. One, two, *three!***

→ *At the audience's noise, Matty jumps into his dad's arms. He screams for an overly long time. After running out of air, Matty calms down and his dad sets him back on the ground.*

MATTY

Might've gotten a little carried away that time.

DAD

Just a smidge.

MATTY

That was Buster, too, wasn't it?

DAD

I'm guessing yes. *(Pause.)* **What's gotten into you, anyway? What are you so scared of?**

MATTY

Every time I close my eyes I see monsters. There's a zombie cowboy in my closet and a fur-covered half-man, half-fly under my bed.

DAD

Well, why don't we check the closet and look under the bed together?

MATTY

It won't help. They're only here when I'm alone.

DAD

Did something happen to scare you?

MATTY

If by "something" you mean "Halloween," then yes.

DAD

Ah, it is that time of year again, isn't it? You're seeing scary stuff everywhere and it's got your brain working overtime.

MATTY

(Shrugs.) **I guess.**

NOISEMAKER

(Loudly whispers to the audience) **On the count of three, everyone whistle and make noises like the wind going through the trees. One, two, *three!***

➡ *At the audience's noises, Matty stiffens, grabs onto his dad, and looks around really scared.*

DAD

It's okay, it's okay. It's just the wind. Matty, didn't we talk about this last year? Remember what we said?

MATTY

You said there's nothing to be afraid of. But that doesn't mean I agreed.

DAD

Well, do you remember what else I said? That when you get scared...

MATTY

I should pray.

DAD

Because...

MATTY

God's with me...so I don't need to be afraid.

DAD

Son, there's all kinds of scary stuff around right now. The other day I saw a house with a skeleton sitting on the front porch. And Mr. Jenkins started wearing that gorilla costume around the neighborhood again. If I didn't know better, I might be afraid myself.

MATTY

You?

DAD

Yes, me. But even though I feel fear, I know I've got a great big God on my side. Half-man, half-fly? Not a chance.

➡ *Just then, Mom enters and taps Dad on the shoulder. He jumps and screams for 30 seconds straight. Mom and Matty stare at him until finally runs out of air, looks at them, and calms down.*

MATTY

God's with you, Dad.

DAD

Thanks, son. I needed that.

NOISEMAKER

(Loudly whispers to the audience) **On the count of three, everyone say "ahhhh." One, two, *three!***

Oh, God Almighty

BEST
Preschool
FOR ....

Kids sing about how God stops all their fears, with fun finger motions and easy words—set to the tune of "The Farmer in the Dell."

....

SCRIPTURE

Isaiah 41:13

Sing It!

When Halloween is here

  (Hands up, fingers open and close)

And scary things appear

  (Hands up, fingers open and close to a neighbor)

Oh, God almighty

  (Lift hands up, fingers open and close)

STOPS all my fear!

  (On "STOPS," hold hands straight out, as if to say, "Stop!")

When scary things appear

  (Hands up, fingers open and close)

God is always near

  (Hands up, fingers open and close to a neighbor)

Oh, God almighty

  (Lift hands up, fingers open and close)

STOPS all my fear!

  (On "STOPS," hold hands straight out, as if to say, "Stop!")

Reverse the Curse

Kids will go trick-or-treating—in reverse!

SCRIPTURE

None

WHAT YOU'LL DO

- candy
- invitations to your ministry
- Bibles to give away (optional)

The Experience

This Halloween, send your kids out with adult chaperones to your church's neighborhood to go trick-or-treating in reverse. Give kids candy and invitations to hand out to residents when they knock on doors. Instead of saying, "Trick-or-treat!" have kids say, "Here's a treat: Jesus loves you!"

As a bonus, in the weeks leading up to Halloween, take up a special collection so you can offer Bibles to residents as well. (Find them for low cost at biblesatcost.com.)

Extra Special FACTOIDS

DID YOU KNOW...

10% of kids prefer gum as a treat on Halloween. 12% of people dress up their pets. 33% of people throw or attend a party, and 46% carve a pumpkin.

DID YOU KNOW...

In 2010, 1.1 *billion* pounds of pumpkins were grown in the U.S. That equals the weight of over 183,000 elephants!
Illinois is responsible for over 1/3 of the total production of pumpkins in the United States.

TRICK or TREAT

THANKSGIVING

GRAVY STUFFING TURKEY Feast PIES MASHED POTATOES

The Bible is full of thanksgiving to God, most notably in the Psalms. The New Testament instructs us to be thankful for everything and at all times. And the Thanksgiving holiday is a great reminder to give God all the praise and thanks he deserves for the blessings he gives us. These activities will help kids express their thanks to God in a variety of hands-on ways.

THANK-FULL

*Kids will learn to live lives
bursting with thankfulness.*

SCRIPTURE

Ephesians 5:20

WHAT YOU'LL NEED

- Bible
- a large balloon for every child

The Experience

Give each child a deflated balloon.

SAY: **Thanksgiving is a time to celebrate all the awesome things we're thankful for. Let's take turns calling out things we're thankful for. Each time someone names something, add a puff of air to your balloon. Ready?**

Let kids name things and add puffs of air to their balloons. After everyone has had a turn, SAY: **Wait, wait, it's my turn!** Call out something unpleasant such as, "Getting sick" or "My car broke down."

SAY: **Hmmm, I'm not sure everyone added air for that one. When good things happen we're all full of praise—like our balloons are now. But when bad things happen, it's more like this.** Have kids release their balloons, letting them fly everywhere and land, deflated.

ASK: **Why don't we thank God when bad things happen?**
Read aloud Ephesians 5:20. Then ASK:

- **Why would God want us to thank him for everything— meaning the good things *and* bad things?**

- **Tell about a time you experienced something good right in the middle of something bad.** Begin by sharing your own story to give kids time to think. For example, you might talk about a time you got a flat tire, but were encouraged by the kindness of someone who helped you.

SAY: **It's easy to thank God for good things. But we can remember to thank God for hard things because often he can use those bad things for good. Let's fill up our balloons so they're nice and full of our praises—for the good stuff and even the not-so-good stuff.** Let kids inflate and tie off their balloons. Help kids tie the balloons as needed.

Lead kids in prayer, thanking God for his blessings of good times and even thanking him for the hard things we face. Then let kids bat the balloons around as a celebration and praise to God.

Warning! To avoid choking hazards, be sure to pick up pieces of any broken balloons promptly. Balloons may contain latex.

Craft

PENNANT POCKETS

BEST
Elementary
FOR
....

Kids raise a victory banner to thank God for what he has done.
....

SCRIPTURE

Exodus 17:8-15

WHAT YOU'LL NEED

- Bible
- felt pennants (assorted colors)
- hole punch
- wooden beads with large holes
- yarn
- felt shapes
- tacky glue
- paper
- pencils

The Experience

SAY: **The Bible tells about a battle that Moses and the Israelites won—but only as long as Moses kept his hands in the air. This was Moses' symbol that he was giving credit to God for the good things God was doing. When the battle was over, listen to what Moses did.** Read Exodus 17:15. **Let's make pennants we can use to lift our praises to God.**

1. Let kids choose two different colored pennants. Help them align the pennants on top of each other and punch holes along the sides about 1 inch apart. Do not hole punch the top (it will be used as a pocket).

2. Give two 4-foot pieces of yarn to the kids.

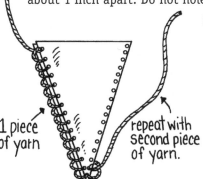

1 piece of yarn

repeat with second piece of yarn.

6 inches   6 inches

3. Keeping the pennants stacked on top of each other, kids can lace one piece of yarn through the holes on one side, looping the yarn around the outside edge of the pennants. Make sure kids leave at least 6 inches of extra yarn on both ends.

4. Repeat on the opposite edge with the second piece of yarn.

5. Have kids create a hanger by tying together the excess of the yarn at the top. Have kids string the bottom pieces of yarn through several beads and then tie a large knot so that the beads won't slip off.

6. Let kids decorate the pennants with felt shapes.

SAY: **When Moses called God his Banner, he was talking about a flag people waved as they marched into battle. He was thanking God for going before them and winning the battle.**

ASK: **What are some ways God has helped you succeed?**

• **How can we remember to thank God when he helps us?**

Distribute paper and pencils, and have kids write thank you notes to God. Then have kids slip the notes in their pennant pockets.

SAY: **Take your pennants home to hang on a doorknob or somewhere in your house. Encourage your family to put thank you notes in the pennant pocket. At Thanksgiving dinner, read the thank you notes with your family as you wave your pennant for God.**

THANKSGIVING

GIFTS FROM ABOVE

BEST FOR All Ages

Kids direct their thanks to the Giver of everything good and perfect.

SCRIPTURE

James 1:17

WHAT YOU'LL NEED

• Bible
• full half-pint water bottles (one per child)
• crepe paper streamers (assorted colors)
• crayons
• string
• thumb tacks

The Experience

Distribute the small water bottles to each child. As kids drink their water, SAY: **Water is one of those things we often take for granted. We drink water every day, and our body needs it to live. But we're so used to having it that we sometimes forget to thank God for something so simple yet important. Thanksgiving is a time we remember to thank God for all of his wonderful gifts.**

Once their water bottles are empty, have kids take off the labels and dry out the inside of the bottles as much as possible.

Set out the colored crepe paper streamers. Have kids tear off small pieces, write or draw something they're thankful for on each piece, crumple the pieces, and place them in their empty water bottles. Challenge kids to fill the bottles with thanks and then replace the caps.

Help kids tie 1-foot strings to the bottlenecks, so at home kids can use thumbtacks to attach the bottles to the ceiling or set them somewhere they pass by every day. Have kids look at the bottles as you read James 1:17.

ASK: **What good and perfect gifts did you thank God for in your bottle?**

• **What reminds you to thank God?**

SAY: **It's easy to forget to thank God. But since the Bible says everything good and perfect comes from God, it's important that we thank him for those many gifts. Take your bottle home and hang it or set it in your house where you'll see it each day. Whenever you look at it, remember to look toward God and thank him.**

Game

I'M STUFFED!

BEST
All Ages
FOR

With a bunch of balloons and oversized T-shirts, kids discover the problem of having too much stuff.

SCRIPTURE

Luke 12:16-21

WHAT YOU'LL NEED

- Bible
- 2 oversized XXL long-sleeve shirts
- balloons

THANKSGIVING

The Experience

Form two teams. Give each group an oversized shirt.

SAY: **Tell whether you think it's good to have a lot of things.** Allow one minute. Then SAY: **Jesus told a story about a rich young man who had lots of things. In fact, he had so many things that he had to keep building bigger and bigger houses to hold it all! Listen.** Read aloud Luke 12:16-19.

SAY: **Let's play a game! Choose one person to wear the oversized shirt. We're going to pretend that your balloons are "things" you can own. When I say "go," inflate your things and stuff them inside the shirt. Whoever has the most things inside the shirt after 60 seconds wins!** For those who can't tie off balloons, suggest that they inflate them while others on their team tie them. Or have a few adult volunteers nearby to help tie.

SAY: **Ready? Go!** After one minute, call time and count the balloons for each team.

SAY: **It might seem like having a lot is a good thing—but listen to how Jesus ends the story.** Read Luke 12:20-21.

ASK: **What's good or bad about owning a lot of things?**

- **Why do you think a relationship with God is more important than things?**

- **What's one way you can show people you believe God is more important than owning a lot of things?**

SAY: **Having a lot of things here on earth can seem like a good thing. After all, you can bless others with your things or give things away to those who need it. But compared to a relationship with God, all of your "things" don't amount to much. A relationship with God is more precious than anything you will ever own.**

Warning! To avoid choking hazards, be sure to pick up pieces of any broken balloons promptly. Balloons may contain latex.

CORNY COBS

BEST
Elementary
FOR
....
*Kids see how fast
thankfulness pops
into their heads.*
....

ALLERGY ALERT
See p. 7

SCRIPTURE

1 Thessalonians 5:18

WHAT YOU'LL NEED

• Bible
• uncooked popcorn
• popcorn machine or
  microwave
• whole graham crackers
• white frosting
• plastic knives

Extra Special
FACTOID

DID YOU KNOW...

Time for a nap? On Thanksgiving
in 2007, people consumed
690 million pounds of turkey
(345,000 tons, mind you)
which equals the weight of 4.48
million people—or the entire
population of Singapore.

The Experience

SAY: **During the first hard year in America, the Pilgrims found corn buried in the sands of Cape Cod. The corn had been stored there by the Native Americans. This important find gave the Pilgrims seeds to plant—and these became the seeds for survival. Without the harvest of corn they reaped from these seeds, the Pilgrims all could've died.**

Corn can remind us to be thankful, too. It's the number one crop in America, and a lot of the food we eat is made with corn—including popcorn!

Start cooking the popcorn. Challenge kids to keep up with the popping by shouting out something they can be thankful for each time they hear a pop.

ASK: **Explain whether it was easy or hard to keep up with the popcorn.**

• How does that compare with how hard it is to keep up with the blessings God gives us in every single day?

Read aloud 1 Thessalonians 5:18.

ASK: **What things make it hard to praise God all the time?**

SAY: **Now let's put our popcorn back together like a corn cob, to remind us that just as popcorn and many other foods come from corn, the good things in our life all come from the same source—God! That's why we can praise him all the time.**

Have kids frost one side of graham crackers, then gently press pieces of popcorn on top the frosting in rows like a corn cob.

Snack

MINI THANKSGIVING

BEST
Elementary
FOR

Kids learn how they can show thankfulness by giving back to God.

THANKSGIVING

ALLERGY ALERT see p. 7

SCRIPTURE

Psalm 136:1-2

WHAT YOU'LL NEED

- Bible
- paper plates
- rolled-up sandwich turkey slices
- Ritz crackers
- Craisins dried fruit
- popcorn
- potato chips
- bread
- celery
- apple slices

The Experience

Before kids arrive, cut bread into smaller squares. Set out all the food.

Have kids wash their hands. <u>SAY</u>: **There are some Thanksgiving foods that are a tradition.**

<u>ASK</u>: **What's your favorite Thanksgiving food?**

<u>SAY</u>: **Some people are so into Thanksgiving food that they call the holiday "Turkey Day" instead! But we know that the name Thanksgiving shows what the holiday is really about: giving thanks.** Read Psalm 136:1-2.

<u>SAY</u>: **We're going to have a mini Thanksgiving dinner. Rather than carved turkey, we've got rolled-up sandwich turkey. For stuffing, we've got bread squares. Popcorn will be our corn, celery our green veggies, and our potatoes will be in chip form. We've also got crackers for rolls and Craisins dried fruit rather than cranberry sauce. We'll finish it off with some apple slices, to remind us of good ol' apple pie.** Hand out plates, and let kids choose from the buffet of mini Thanksgiving snacks.

Have kids sit in a circle. As kids eat their snacks, go around the circle as many times as possible and have kids share one thing they're thankful for.

Close with this prayer: **Dear God, you've given us so much. Our big Thanksgiving meals celebrate all that you've given us. We want to give our thanks back to you. Please help us remember to always say thank you. In Jesus' name, amen.**

A TALE OF TWO THANKSGIVINGS

A hard-hitting drama about being truly thankful.

SCRIPTURE

1 Thessalonians 5:18

PROPS

- a table with a nice tablecloth and centerpiece
- an old, broken down, cheap-looking table

CAST

- Ruby, dressed very nicely in a pretty dress
- James, dressed humbly (jeans and a plain shirt)
- Mom

BEHIND THE SCENES

For this skit, a simple setup of two tables is all that's necessary. You can decorate the nicer table with place settings, but it's not vital to the meaning of the skit.

Action!

➡️ *On the stage, we see two tables. The table on the left side has a tablecloth and a nice centerpiece. The table on the right side is old, broken down, and cheap-looking. Ruby is standing near the nicer table. James is standing near the old table.*

RUBY

Mother, I can't believe you expect me to spend the day in this dress. It's too itchy and the tag jabs me in the neck. *(She pulls it out and looks at it.)* **No wonder. The price tag. Huh. No wonder it feels so cheap—it was only $200.**

JAMES

God, I know you can hear me up there. And I know today is Thanksgiving, so I'm supposed to be saying thanks, but I wondered if I could ask a favor...

RUBY

And they messed up my manicure at the salon! It's a good thing they didn't talk back when I refused to pay for it.

JAMES

Mom's at work and she's trying to get off early. We don't have money for a big turkey or anything, but I made some mac 'n cheese, and the only thing I really want is for Mom to have the afternoon off so we can eat together. She works so hard, God.

RUBY

Cranberries again? And sweet potatoes? Ick. No one ever eats them. And the mashed potatoes are so lumpy. You really should've used more milk. I wouldn't eat that if you paid me.

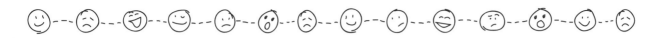

JAMES

I know it's not fancy, but I don't want to make any more mess for Mom. I know she's going to make it home. I just know it.

RUBY

And I'm sitting by cousin Ben? He smells, Mother. Don't tell me you haven't noticed. Can we put deodorant at his place setting? We'd be doing him a favor.

JAMES

I found some leftover Halloween candy in my room. I thought we could save that for dessert. I've got it all planned out, God. I just need Mom to walk through that door. But I know even if she doesn't, I have so much to be thankful for. She loves me, and she taught me about you. That makes me the luckiest kid in the world.

RUBY

I hope your apple pie doesn't taste like it did the last time you made it. It was all dry and flaky—and not in a good way. And did you buy the expensive ice cream? I don't want that cheap grocery store brand.

➡ *On James' side of the stage, his mother enters. She's carrying a rolled-up brown paper sack and smiling.*

MOM

James, Mr. Johnson let me out early. He said he could send one of us home and just felt like it should be me. Do you believe it? He even gave me some leftovers—we're going to have a real turkey dinner and apple pie for dessert!

RUBY

(Crosses her arms in a huff.) Thanksgiving is such a lame holiday.

JAMES

I'm just so glad you're here, Mom. *(He hugs her.)* This is the best Thanksgiving ever.

I AM THANKFUL

BEST
Preschool
FOR
....

A fun song about being thankful, set to the tune of "Frère Jacques."

....

SCRIPTURE

Psalm 107:8-9

Sing It!

I am thankful

(Sign for "Thank You": move right hand from chin to palm of other hand)

I am thankful

(Sign for "Thank You": move right hand from chin to palm of other hand)

To my God

(Point up)

To my God

(Point up)

For his many blessings

(Hands on heart)

Turkey and the dressings

(Hands on stomach)

Thank you, God!

(Sign for "Thank You": move right hand from chin to palm of other hand.)

Thank you, God!

(Sign for "Thank You": move right hand from chin to palm of other hand.)

JUST FOR FUN...

Why can't you take a turkey to church?

Because its language is so fowl.

If April showers bring May flowers, what do May flowers bring?

Pilgrims.

WALL OF THANKS

BEST
Elementary
FOR

Kids will give thanks as they point out what God does for all of us.

SCRIPTURE

1 Chronicles 16:8

WHAT YOU'LL NEED

- Bible
- roll of butcher paper or newsprint
- ink pads
- wet wipes
- sticky notes
- markers
- Now & Later candies

The Experience

Contact a local mall or shopping center about hosting a "Thanks Wall" around the week of Thanksgiving, especially on busy shopping days such as Black Friday.

Gather kids together, and read 1 Chronicles 16:8. <u>SAY:</u> **This Thanksgiving, we're going to help our community see what God has done for us by giving thanks.** Have kids make the wall by using an ink pad to make handprints all over a long piece of butcher paper or newsprint. Decorate a headline that reads, "We're thankful for…"

Hang the Thanks Wall at the designated location, and have a few kids at a time stand with adult volunteers in shifts. Set out sticky note pads and markers. Encourage people to write what they're thankful for on a note and stick it to the backdrop. Hand out Now & Later candies to people who write on the wall and say, "Remember to give thanks now…and later!"

THANKSGIVING

FLOCK OF TURKEYS

BEST FOR All Ages

Kids will hang turkeys as they collect money to provide Thanksgiving meals for the hungry in your area.

SCRIPTURE

Isaiah 58:10

WHAT YOU'LL NEED

- Bible
- copies of the handout on page 156

The Experience

Many cities have rescue missions that collect money for Thanksgiving dinners. Often, a very small donation buys a full Thanksgiving meal for someone. Find a rescue mission in your area to find out how much it costs to provide one meal. Copy the image of the turkey from the handout on page 156.

SAY: **Thanksgiving is a harvest celebration, a way to thank God for providing food for the winter by way of a great harvest in the fall. But not everyone has a lot of food to eat. Some people don't have very much at all.**

Read aloud Isaiah 58:10. SAY: **This Thanksgiving, let's collect money for people who don't have a place to eat a Thanksgiving dinner.**

Tell kids about the rescue mission you've selected and how much it costs to feed one person a Thanksgiving meal there. Encourage kids to bring in donations for the rescue mission. Hang a turkey on the wall each time kids have raised enough for one meal.

Extra Special FACTOID

DID YOU KNOW...

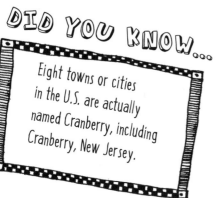

Eight towns or cities in the U.S. are actually named Cranberry, including Cranberry, New Jersey.

Christmas

Merry Christmas

For lots of people, Christmas is associated with shopping, presents, stress, busyness, and Santa. But the Bible introduces a simple, humble first Christmas centered around a baby in a manger. This baby, Jesus, came from heaven as the Savior of the world. Amid the hubbub that Christmas encompasses today, you can bring your kids back to the humble beginnings of Christmas and point them to Jesus with these activities.

Eyes on Jesus

BEST
Elementary
FOR

Kids search for a partner as they experience how the wise men searched for Jesus.

SCRIPTURE

Matthew 2:8-12

WHAT YOU'LL NEED

• Bible

The Experience

Have kids stand in a circle. You'll need an even number of kids in the circle, so decide whether or not to participate based on how many kids you have.

SAY: **It's Christmas, and we're celebrating Jesus' birth. Today we're learning about how the wise men searched to find baby Jesus. Let's experience what it's like to search for someone right now.**

Gather kids in a circle facing each other.

SAY: **You're going to close your eyes. When I say, "Search out!" open your eyes and look out across the circle and try to lock eyes with someone.** Let kids practice.

Now let's play. When I tell you to search out, if the person you look at is looking back at you, run to the center of the circle and celebrate finding each other with a high five; then move outside the circle as a pair. If you're looking at someone who's looking at someone else, then stay in our circle for another round and close your eyes again.

Repeat until all the kids are in pairs. Then have kids discuss the following questions with their partners.

ASK: **Describe what it was like trying to lock eyes with a partner.**

• **Talk about a time you looked really hard for something—and then you found it.**

SAY: **To lock eyes with someone, you had to focus, act quickly, and pay attention. Let's see what the wise men did to "lock eyes" with baby Jesus.**

Read aloud Matthew 2:8-12.

ASK: **How were the wise men focused on baby Jesus?**

SAY: **The wise men searched for baby Jesus. They followed the star in the east to find him. When the wise men found Jesus, they were filled with joy. They knelt down in front of him and worshipped him.**

ASK: **At Christmas, what kinds of things take your attention away from Jesus?**

• **Why do you think stores and ads seem to focus on everything *except* Jesus?**

• **What are ways you can stay focused on Jesus at Christmas?**

SAY: **This Christmas we can celebrate the joy of baby Jesus, too. We can keep our focus on him.**

PRAY: **Dear God, thank you for sending Jesus. Help us keep our eyes on him—today and every day. In Jesus' name, amen.**

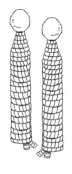
Mini Manger

Kids create a crafty mini nativity that makes a delightful decoration.

SCRIPTURE

Luke 2:6-7

WHAT YOU'LL NEED

- Bible
- assorted yarns
- wooden, flat-ended round doll pins
- ½-inch wooden furniture plugs*
- ½x1-inch wooden shaker pegs*
- white glue
- hot glue gun
- wooden, colonial-style napkin rings*
- Spanish moss

*available at craft stores

The Experience

Read aloud Luke 2:6-7.

ASK: **What do you think that first Christmas looked like?**

• **What are your favorite ways to decorate for Christmas?**

SAY: **The way people decorate for Christmas is often a lot fancier than the inside of a barn, which is where Jesus was born. We're going to make our very own simple Christmas decorations today that show what happened in the verses we read.**

1. Give each child two round doll pins, one furniture plug, one shaker peg, and one napkin ring. Have kids glue the ½-inch furniture plug to the bottom of one of the round doll pins. This pin represents Joseph. The other doll pin will represent Mary, and the shaker peg will represent baby Jesus.

2. Using white glue to stick the yarn to the pins, have kids wrap each doll pin and the shaker peg with different colors of yarn, leaving the heads exposed.

3. With hot glue, help kids glue the Mary and Joseph pins together and then glue them to the outside of the napkin ring so they are all level on the bottom.

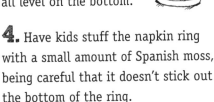

4. Have kids stuff the napkin ring with a small amount of Spanish moss, being careful that it doesn't stick out the bottom of the ring.

5. Help kids hot glue the shaker peg Jesus to the top of the Spanish moss inside the napkin ring. The kids now have their very own mini manger scene!

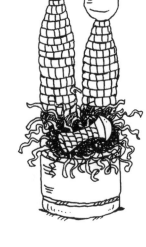

Poinsettia Christmas Trees

BEST
FOR All Ages

As kids press poinsettia leaves into the shape of Christmas trees, they'll learn how Christmas trees can point us to Jesus.

SCRIPTURE

Matthew 2:1-2

WHAT YOU'LL NEED

- Bible
- poinsettia plants
- wax paper
- hand towel
- iron
- ironing board
- silver glitter glue

The Experience

Show kids a poinsettia flower. Point out the star shape of each flower. SAY: **Poinsettias are often used to decorate for Christmas because they're great winter plants. And the star shape of the flower reminds us of the first Christmas star.** Read aloud Matthew 2:1-2.

ASK: **What are other places you see stars around Christmas?**

SAY: **Another place we see the Christmas star is on a Christmas tree. There's a story from hundreds of years ago that tells of a Christian named Martin Luther. He went for a walk in the woods around Christmas and noticed how the snow shimmered on the branches of the evergreen trees. It reminded him of a shining star, pointing us to heaven. So he took a tree home and decorated it for Christmas.**

Let's use poinsettias and Christmas trees to make a fun craft that points us to Jesus.

Give each child two pieces of wax paper.

Have kids pick leaves and petals off the poinsettia and arrange them in the shape of a Christmas tree on one piece of wax paper. When kids are done arranging, have them set their wax papers on the ironing board and place their second piece of wax paper on top.

Iron each child's wax paper, first setting the hand towel on the craft and then ironing evenly on medium dry heat. The heat will seal the wax paper together, preserving the kids' arrangements.

Let kids decorate their wax paper creations with silver glitter glue to make the branches shimmer the way Martin Luther observed.

ASK: **What will you do this Christmas to stay focused on Jesus?**

Have kids hold up their crafts. SAY: **Our Christmas trees help us remember Jesus in another way, too. They're pointy at the top, like an arrow pointing us to heaven. This Christmas, make sure your celebrations all point to Jesus!**

Game

Count Your Chickens

BEST
All Ages
FOR

Animal sounds abound in
this fun Christmas game!

WHAT YOU'LL NEED

• no supplies needed

The Experience

In a large group, number kids 1 through 5, and ask them to remember their numbers. SAY: **Baby Jesus was born in a stable. A stable is a place where animals eat and sleep. And wouldn't you know...in our stable, the animals have all escaped!** Have kids spread out around the room. Assign animals to the numbers 1 through 5. For example, all of the 1's are cows, the 2's are horses, the 3's are chickens, and so on. Choose animals that make distinctive sounds. Explain that kids must get on all fours, close their eyes, and locate their group just by listening to and making the animal sounds.

SAY: **Ready? Go!** Allow time for all the kids to find their groups.

When the "animals" are all grouped together, SAY: **Now, I don't know if there were actually cows and chickens at Jesus' birth, but I do know who was there. Shepherds, wise men—even angels. What a great way to celebrate a birthday!** Have "animal" groups discuss the following:

- **How do you celebrate your birthday?**
- **What are some ways you celebrate Jesus' birthday?**
- **Why is it important to celebrate Jesus' birth?**

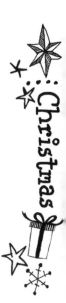

Christmas

Extra Special
FACTOID

DID YOU KNOW...

The first artificial Christmas trees were made in Germany. They were made of goose feathers that had been dyed green.

Good News Angel

This snack comes bearing good news that'll bring great joy to all people!

SCRIPTURE

Luke 2:8-14

ALLERGY
See p. 7
ALERT

WHAT YOU'LL NEED

- Bible
- round waffles
- mini-round waffles
- raisins or chocolate chips
- banana slices
- orange slices
- powdered sugar
- syrup
- large paper plates
- napkins
- plastic knives
- forks
- condiment cups for syrup

The Experience

Toast or cook the waffles in advance. If possible, keep the waffles warm for kids.

SAY: **It's Christmas, and we're celebrating the birth of Jesus.**

ASK: **What's something you know about Christmas?**

- **How did you learn those things?**

SAY: **Let's see how people first found out Jesus was born.** Read aloud Luke 2:8-12. **Let's make angels appear right now to remind us of the good news that Jesus was born.**

1. Set out the snack supplies.

2. Have kids place the large round waffle on the plate and carefully cut an inch-wide half-circle from each side to form two wings.

3. Adjust the wings so there's a small space between each wing and the angel's body.

4. Have kids place the mini waffle above the body on the plate to make the head.

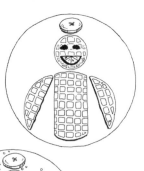

5. Add raisins or chocolate chips for eyes and an orange slice for a mouth.

6. Use a banana slice for a halo.

7. Have kids dust the angel with powdered sugar.

8. Hand out forks. Serve with an individual cup of syrup for dunking.

After kids have made their angels, have kids make the orange slice mouths move as you read Luke 2:14.

ASK: **Describe a time that something amazing happened to you. Who did you tell about it?**

- **What can you do to spread the good news of Jesus like the angels did?**

SAY: **The angels delivered some pretty amazing news to the shepherds. Later, the shepherds passed on the news, too! We can continue passing on the good news of the great joy of Jesus' birth.**

Tip

Cut raisins in half for kids under 4.

Find-and-Eat Christmas Story

BEST
Elementary
FOR

With this edible nativity, kids experience the Christmas story in a delicious way!

ALLERGY
see p. 7
ALERT

SCRIPTURE

Luke 2:1-20; Matthew 2:1-11

WHAT YOU'LL NEED

- Bible
- resealable sandwich bags
- 9 bowls
- white chocolate-covered pretzels
- mini marshmallows
- 3 flavors of Teddy Grahams
- gummy bears
- pretzel nuggets
- golden raisins
- pretzel sticks
- raisins
- animal crackers
- plates

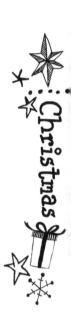

Christmas

The Experience

Place each ingredient in a bowl and set up an assembly line for kids to create their snacks. You can arrange the ingredients in any order in the assembly line.

SAY: **You're going to create your snack today by placing one of each item in your bag. When you get to the gummy bears and Teddy Grahams, take three of each of those.**

Have kids go through the assembly line, each putting the following in a bag. Monitor the line, helping kids remember to take extra Teddy Grahams and gummy bears.

1 white chocolate-covered pretzel
1 mini marshmallow
3 Teddy Grahams
3 different-colored gummy bears
1 pretzel nugget
1 golden raisin
1 pretzel stick
1 raisin
1 animal cracker

Distribute plates. Open your Bible to Luke 2:1-20 and show kids the words. SAY: **It's Christmas, and we're celebrating Jesus' birth. Let's experience the true story of how Jesus was born with our tasty treats. As I tell the Christmas story, find the ingredient I show you in your "Find-and-Eat Treat" and set it on your plate.**

Hold up a gummy bear, and have kids find theirs. **A long time ago, an angel visited a young girl named Mary.** Hold up the white chocolate covered pretzel and have kids to find the angel. **The angel told Mary that she was going to have a baby, and that the baby would be named Jesus.**

A little while later, Mary married a man named Joseph. Hold up a second gummy bear, and have kids find theirs. **Joseph and Mary had to travel to the town of Bethlehem to pay a tax.** Have kids make the two gummy bears "walk."

When Joseph and Mary arrived in Bethlehem, there was no place for them to stay. Finally an inn-keeper told Joseph that they could stay in his stable with the animals.

Hold up an animal cracker, and have kids find theirs. **Mary and Joseph rested among the animals.** Have kids demonstrate with their gummy bears and animal cracker. **Then Mary had her baby.** Have kids find the third gummy bear. **They wrapped Jesus in a blanket and put him in a manger.** Have kids find the pretzel nugget and place their third gummy bear on it.

Nearby in the hills some shepherds tending flocks noticed a bright light in the sky. Have kids find the mini marshmallow. **An angel appeared and told them that Jesus, the Son of God, was born.** Have kids make the white chocolate covered pretzel hover over the marshmallow. **The shepherds went to Bethlehem to see the baby Jesus.** Have kids each lead their mini marshmallow to the pretzel nugget manger.

Far away, three wise men saw a bright star in the sky. Have kids find their three Teddy Grahams. **The wise men followed the star to see what they could find. The bright star led them to the baby Jesus.** Have kids "walk" the Teddy Grahams to the pretzel nugget manger. **The wise men knelt down and worshipped the baby Jesus. They gave Jesus presents of gold, frankincense, and myrrh.** Have kids set their golden raisin, pretzel stick, and raisin between the Teddy Grahams and the pretzel nugget.

Have kids arrange their snack however they'd like to depict the nativity scene. Then let them eat up as you discuss the following questions.

ASK: **What was your favorite part of our snack?**

• **What is sweet to you about Christmas?**

SAY: **Mary and Joseph can teach us to obey God no matter what. The angels and shepherds show us how to spread the good news. And the wise men show us how to worship Jesus. This Christmas, look for ways to obey, tell about, and worship Jesus.**

This Is the Son God Gave

BEST
All Ages
FOR

An interactive skit, where kids experience how Jesus was sent to earth to "untangle" our sins—and how he is a light of hope in the darkness of the world.

SCRIPTURE

Luke 2:1-20

PROPS

- 3 strings of Christmas lights
- an extension cord, with one end plugged into a wall outlet

CAST

- Narrator
- 3 Group Leaders

BEHIND THE SCENES

Plug one end of the extension cord into a wall outlet. Have the audience form three groups, each led by a Group Leader and holding a string of Christmas lights. (Test the lights beforehand to make sure they work.) If you have a large audience, create more groups, add Group Leaders, and add strings of Christmas lights.

Action!

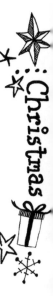

➡ *The Narrator begins center stage. He or she has the audience form three separate groups. Have groups sit and then hand each a string of Christmas lights. Have groups unroll the lights so everyone in the group is holding onto a part of the strand.*

NARRATOR

This is the Son that God gave.

➡ *Group One stands, holding its string of lights with the Group Leader at the front of the line.*

NARRATOR

Mary's the mom, who had the Son that God gave.

➡ *Group Two stands, holding its string of lights with the Group Leader at the front of the line.*

NARRATOR

Joe is the dad, who married the mom, who had the Son that God gave.

➡ *Group Three stands, holding its string of lights with the Group Leader at the front of the line. All three groups, led by the Group Leaders, start to cross each other's lines, ducking and weaving in and out, beginning to tangle up the lines and strings of Christmas lights. The Group Leaders will stop at the end of each of the Narrator's lines.*

NARRATOR

This is the town, where Joseph was from, who's also the dad, who married the mom, who had the Son that God gave.

➡ *All three groups stop, and the Narrator pauses. The Group Leaders begin moving again when the Narrator starts speaking. This happens on every one of the Narrator's lines.*

NARRATOR

This is the inn, the inn in the town, where Joseph was from, who's also the dad, who married the mom, who had the Son that God gave.

➡ *Groups stop, Narrator pauses, groups begin again on Narrator's line.*

NARRATOR

There was a man who ran the inn, the inn in the town, where Joseph was from, who's also the dad, who married the mom, who had the Son that God gave.

➡ *Groups stop, Narrator pauses, groups begin again on Narrator's line.*

NARRATOR

This is the barn, a stable of sorts, owned by the man who ran the inn. Remember the inn? The inn in the town, where Joseph was from, who's also the dad, who married the mom, who had the Son that God gave.

➡ *Groups stop, Narrator pauses, groups begin again on Narrator's line.*

NARRATOR

This is the cow that mooed in the barn, a stable of sorts, owned by the man who ran the inn. Remember the inn? The inn in the town, where Joseph was from, who's also the dad, who married the mom, who had the Son that God gave.

➡ *Pause for a moment, and have kids look around at their tangled mess. The Group Leaders don't move this time.*

NARRATOR

The reason that God sent Jesus to earth was not because he was bored.
The reason that God sent Jesus to earth was because earth needed a Lord.

Pause.
So...in the barn, a baby was born!

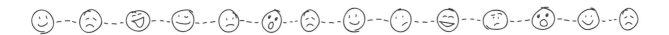

GROUP LEADERS

(To their groups) **Repeat after me, "Jesus was born!"**

AUDIENCE/LEADERS/ NARRATOR

Jesus was born! Jesus was born!

➡ *When the Narrator continues, Group Leaders and kids, without letting go of their Christmas lights, start to unravel and untangle to get back to their groups on the Narrator's cue.*

NARRATOR

**Time to untangle, from head to toe!
Ready? Steady? Here we go!
Jesus was born! Next to the cow! Born in the barn! Remember the barn? A stable of sorts, owned by the man. Remember the man? He ran the inn. Remember the inn? The inn in the town, where Joseph was from, who's also the dad, who married the mom, who had the Son that God gave.**

➡ *Once the groups are untangled and back to their groups, have Group Leaders plug their Christmas lights into each other's. The Narrator holds one end of an extension cord that is plugged into a wall outlet. If possible, turn out all the lights in the room.*

NARRATOR

**The people on earth looked like you did just now—
A bewildered, tangled-up jumble.
But Jesus, God's Son, in swaddling cloth curled,
As angels and shepherds and praises all swirled,
Proclaimed that this baby would be the light of the world** *(Plug in lights)*
And save us all from our sins.

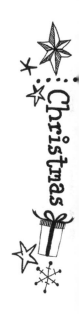

Jesus, Our Savior

BEST *Preschool* **FOR**

A song about Jesus' birth, sung to the tune of "Pop! Goes the Weasel."

SCRIPTURE

Luke 2

Sing It!

All the way from Bethlehem

(Kids raise right arm to make one side of a "house" shape)

To end up in a stable

(Kids raise left arm to complete the "house" shape)

He was born on Christmas Day

(Kids bring hands down, palms up)

Jesus, our Savior!

(Kids raise hands over their heads, palms up.)

Mary and Joseph

(Kids wave right hand, keep it up)

Wise men and the angels

(Kids wave left hand, keep it up)

They all came to see God's Son

(Kids bring hands down, palms up)

Jesus, our Savior!

(Kids raise hands over their heads, palms up.)

JUST FOR FUN...

What did Adam say on December 24th?

"It's Christmas, Eve!"

Welcome Home

BEST Elementary FOR

Jesus made the earth his home, and kids will help make their town a welcoming home for new residents.

SCRIPTURE

John 1:14

WHAT YOU'LL NEED

- list of contact information for city buildings, post offices, libraries, and so on
- markers
- dry-erase board and markers
- mailing labels
- manila envelopes
- church brochures
- local business coupons (optional)

The Experience

Prepare ahead by contacting a realtors association to get an idea of how many people move to the area from out of town each month or year. Print that many copies of phone numbers and addresses of important places like city buildings, post offices, libraries, grocery stores and utility companies. Leave room at the bottom of the page. Also print information about your Christmas services on mailing labels.

With kids, read John 1:14. <u>SAY:</u> **Jesus came to earth in a stable, with cloths for blankets and shepherds as the welcoming committee. Even though a barn isn't the most cozy place to call home, he had people around to make his home on earth welcoming. Let's do the same thing for new people in our town. To welcome them, we'll make some welcome packets.**

First, have kids vote on their favorite restaurants, parks, and other places to go. Write the winning two votes of each category on a dry-erase board. Distribute the copies of the phone number and address sheet and have kids write at the bottom, "We also recommend:" with the names of places that won the most votes.

Then have kids decorate manila envelopes with phrases such as "Welcome to our town!" or "Get to know your new home!" Kids can also decorate the envelopes with wreaths, Christmas trees, ornaments, stars, and other Christmas pictures. Fill manila envelopes with one address sheet and a church brochure per envelope. Include information about your church services by printing the information on a mailing label and sticking it on your church brochure. Have kids hold the envelopes and pray for the people who'll receive them.

You may also contact local businesses such as fast food restaurants, pizza parlors, salons, and grocery stores for coupons to put in the packets.

Ask real estate companies and schools to keep the packets to hand out to new residents, or post them on community bulletin boards.

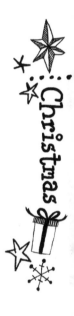

Christmas

Treasure Jars

Kids help new mothers treasure their infants, just as Mary did.

....

SCRIPTURE

Luke 2:19

WHAT YOU'LL NEED

- Bible
- clean jars
- patterned contact paper
- mailing labels
- baby-themed stickers
- index cards
- pens

The Experience

Read Luke 2:19. <u>SAY:</u> **A lot of moms treasure their new babies in the same way. Let's give new moms a special gift by making them Treasure Jars.** Have each child choose a clean jar to decorate with colorful contact paper. Have kids write "Treasure Jar" on a mailing label and stick it on the jar. Kids can add baby-themed stickers to the contact paper for extra decoration. Encourage older kids to add Luke 2:11-12 or another message about Jesus' birth.

Have kids each start out the jar with treasuring thoughts written on an index card by completing sentences such as

"My wish for you is..."

"You are blessed because..."

"Your life is special because..."

"I hope you feel..."

Then fill each jar with blank index cards and a pen, placing the pre-written cards on top.

Contact your local hospital and ask about placing the jars where new moms can each take one to record their thoughts and memories of their babies' first days.

Extra Special FACTOID

DID YOU KNOW...

If you received every present in the song "The 12 Days of Christmas," you'd have a total of 364 presents.

Handouts

FATHER'S DAY SYMBOLS

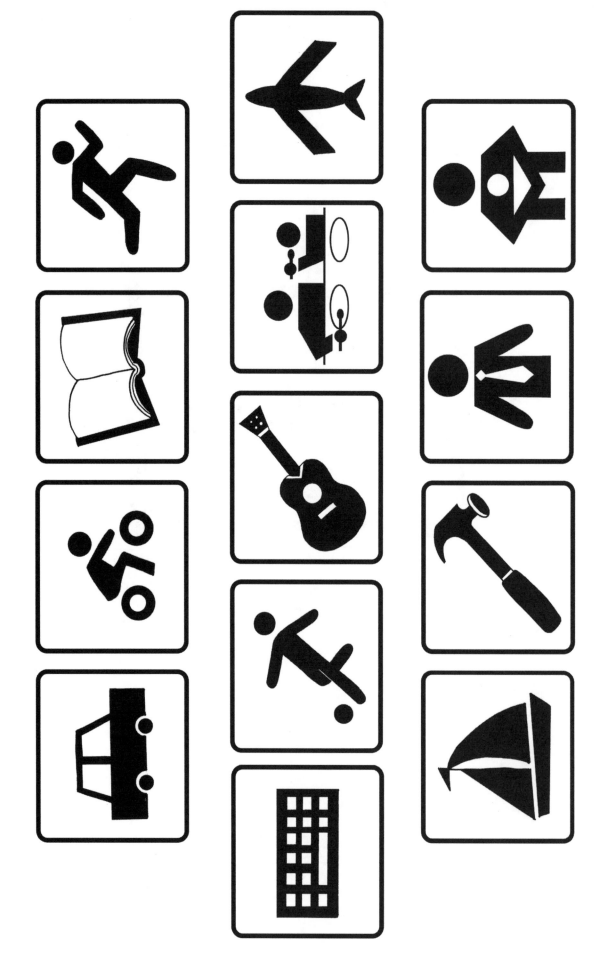

PEEK-A-BOO DAD SYMBOLS

TREASURE TIES

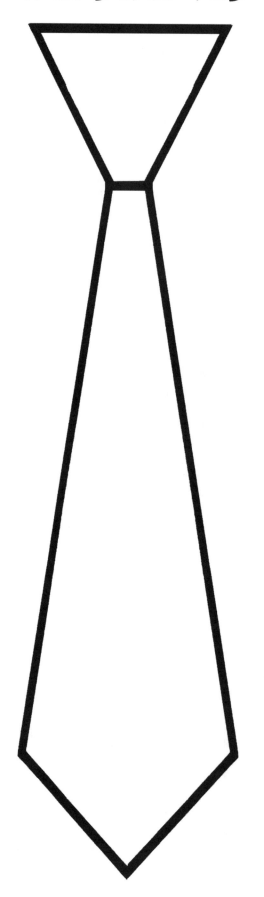

Optical Illusion

Index

Practical ideas to give
your ministry
a boost!

Children's Ministry Magazine
Ideas and Inspiration for Your Ministry

With Children's Ministry Magazine, you get:

- Authentic ministry ideas to **help change children's lives**
- Advice from today's ministry experts and veterans to **keep you motivated and inspired**
- Innovative tips to create a program that will **have kids begging to come back**

**Get your risk-free trial issue today at
childrensministry.com or call 800.447.1070**